Director of Photography:
Charles M. Rafshoon

with Algimantas Kezys

Word Books, Publisher
Waco, Texas

The Search for JIMMY CARTER

Tom Collins

Printed in the United States of America.

ISBN #87680–820–8
Library of Congress catalog number: 76-27221

Contents

Part 1   Jimmy Country   13
In which a stranger visits the presidential homeland and attempts to find where the bodies are buried, to discover who did what to whom, and to dig around and locate the wellsprings of this particular Jimmy Carter kind of life force and energy.

Part 2   Country Jimmy   69
In which the outsider shuffles through files containing the strange enough story of a peanut breeder's progress to the Georgia governorship, emerging in a few years, before the startled gaze of the populace, with a presidential nomination; all of which leads to the dizzying conclusion that there seems to be now no way defeat can be seized from the jaws of previous victories.

Part 3   Who Is Jimmy Carter?   149
In which the visitor attempts to explore some of the bizarre questions that have been raised or willy-nilly must be raised, concerning the most extraordinary candidacy that has occurred in a very long while: questions spiritual and political, emotional and psychiatric—innocent, insolent and weird questions, about experience and innocence, sincerity and deception, cunning and compassion, about intelligence and unremitting toil, about love and anger and personal morality, relentless ambition and religious faith.

Acknowledgments

My grateful thanks to Patricia Collins, above all; to Lillian Carter, who shared so very generously of her time and vast experience; to Pam Law, the greatest midnight oil burner of them all, who typed 160,000 words of transcripts and other confidential material; to Floyd Thatcher, Ron Patterson, and Dennis Hill for their patience, professionalism, and above all their imagination. To Mulkey McMichael, who so enthusiastically did so much of the work of laying out and preparing the book; to Jane Mary Farley, who helped structure it; to Paul Fuqua, who brought the Mountain to Mahomet; to Charles Rafshoon, who knew things and opened avenues of inquiry; to Rosalynn Carter, whose sensitivity and intelligence were an inspiration throughout the whole endeavor; to Gladys Crabb, as thoughtful and encouraging an editor as can be found anywhere; to John and Betty Pope, who offered many kindnesses, and their hospitality as well; to Maxine Reese, Chief Town Rabbi of Plains, Georgia, and her vaudeville partner, Pattie Price Pearson, both of whom spoke from their hearts; to Dick Pettys, Peter Pringle, Wes Pippert, Jim Wooten, Bill Wyant & Lynn Olson, and the many other lords and ladies of the media, who provided questions, wisdom, and refreshment; to Mr. S. S. Crowe & Co., who by furnishing protection insured the welfare of all concerned; to Betty Mayo, for her counsel; to Oliver Miller, one of the most thoughtful and considerate people on the Carter staff; to Al Kezys, who gathered images and spread happiness; to Joan Daniel, who loved her work; to Marion McReynolds, who flew in to help lift the secretarial burden; to Doug Gatian, who did all that he was asked to do, and more; and to all the many people who offered and gave their help, among them Joyce Buckner, Ron Ranew, Shirley Goodin, Betty Lusk, Ken Drew, George Combs, Tim Johnson, Kim Kelly, and especially Mary Ruth Howes.

Tom Collins
August 1976

Part 1
Jimmy Country

In which a stranger visits the presidential homeland and attempts to find where the bodies are buried, to discover who did what to whom, and to dig around and locate the wellsprings of this particular Jimmy Carter kind of life force and energy.

Jimmy Country may be variously approached. One way is to take a limousine (actually a panel van) from Hartsfield Airport outside Atlanta to the Continental Trailways depot in the center of the city, and then board a bus for Americus and Albany in South Georgia. A Northeasterner may be startled by highway signs on the road out of Atlanta evoking Civil War memories—Chattanooga, Stone Mountain, Andersonville.

Moving down Highway 19, one passes near the mythical Tara of GONE WITH THE WIND and the very real hog farm that used to belong to U.S. Senator Herman Talmadge, son of Gene Talmadge. To see Gene Talmadge, when he was Governor of Georgia in the thirties and forties was— for a farmer from South Georgia—like to seein' the face of God. When the farmer died, he would go to Atlanta to see Gene. A fellow traveler, a native Georgian, laughs and tells you more about Gene. "Talmadge would have on a $250 suit and be riding in the finest limousine that his time could afford, and he would get to the edge of a small town like Buena Vista and change into his old work trousers held up by red galluses, and walk into the town, get on a tree stump—always an actual stump of a tree—and scream 'of how the evil nigger folk is trying to take over and kill all the white people.' After everything was over and all the locals had gone home, Gene would get back into his $250 suit, climb into his limousine, laugh about what fools he had made of those stupid rednecks, and ride to the next town. He'd do the same thing all day long. The people loved it."

Most days, if you are on the 3:35 p.m. bus, and if you have Tommy Reeves as your driver, he will tell you that he has had Jimmy and Rosalynn Carter as passengers, exhausted and sometimes asleep after a hard night's day on the campaign trail. And he's had Jimmy's mother, Miz Lillian, as a passenger, too. She is far more talkative, he says, than her son Jimmy. Tommy's been carrying her for a long while; she sometimes traveled with him back and forth when she was visiting Jimmy in Atlanta during his sojourn there as Governor of Georgia (1971 to 1975).

The countryside is pleasant enough and even lush; but Tommy will tell you that times were hard in the days gone by in South Georgia, which on this road begins, more or less, just above Ellaville. He bounces the bus along through one stretch of steeply sloping up-and-down road; you ask him about the hills, and he says that the main purpose of this part of Georgia is to keep the rest of the world zippered together.

Nothing Tommy Reeves says in his soft Georgia drawl sounds at all illiberal. "Liberal" or "illiberal"—such words do not come easily to the tongue down here; nor does "conservative." But Reeves seems to be a man open to experience and possibilities. You note that he calls himself "Tommy." The man from South Georgia who refused to lie down and settle for the vice-presidency as a ticket-balancer, is called simply "Jimmy" by the people down here. His thirty-eight-year-old brother—who now seems to be the leading full-time male resident of Plains, Georgia—is called "Billy." There are other Billys there, but in a South Georgia

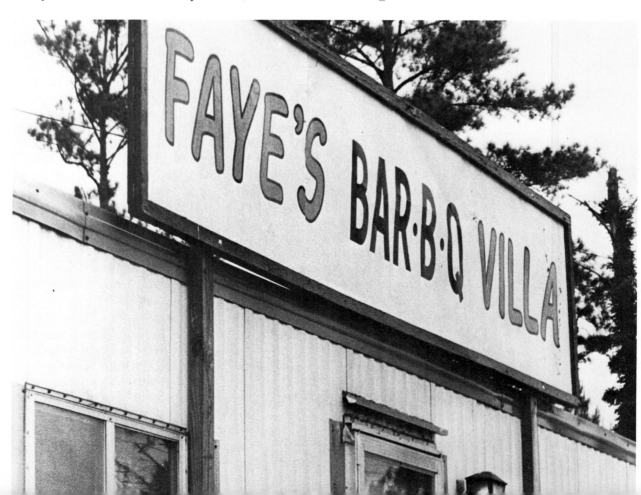

town, a leading citizen, so far from gathering further honorifics, finds that his patronymic is ignored and that he is reduced, or elevated, to the status of one-name recognition.

Anyway, after the bus has rested itself in Butler for fifteen minutes, Tommy Reeves takes the wheel again and winds his way on down till he finally drops you at the bus depot in the "Georgia certified city" of Americus, in Sumter County. Now it used to be said by people in the area that Plains was nine miles from Americus. Today, of course, it is said by people in Washington that Americus is nine miles from Plains and that Atlanta is 134 miles from Americus.

Supposing you've rented a car for the short trip from Americus to Plains. If it's a Hertz, that means Randy Jones's gas station, at the corner of Cotton and Forsyth. Mr. Jones is a pleasant, stump-like man who seems heavily pre-occupied with the light paper work on his office desk. From nowhere appears a somewhat thinner and shorter stump, with a high-pitched voice, who looks like at least a cousin of Truman Capote. Don Dailey is his name; "Shorty," he says amiably, "is what they call me." Shorty fills the tank and checks out the car. A turn down the block and you are back again. Mr. Jones explains that the seemingly faulty steering on the vehicle is probably due to lack of air in the tires. Shorty checks the tires. "No problem there," he says cheerfully. Taking the steering wheel of the rented car, and your life, in your hands, you head back west a few blocks to where U.S. 19, along with Georgia Highway 280, splits south. You continue on to the Best Western Motel.

If it's a warm evening in Americus, and you've decided that the thing to do is eat supper (never "dinner" at night down here), there is a place really worth visiting. A few inquiries will send you back north along the highway, maybe three quarters of a mile. At a Phillips 66 station you turn off onto a little road. There at your immediate left is a prefab shambles called Faye's Bar-B-Q Villa. Though it is the barbecue that is advertised, tonight only great steak is served and eaten. Faye West, a smiling and bemused brunette, prepares everything except the meat. She has a sweet potato soufflé and a bleu cheese dressing which would be pleasant to find anywhere. Her husband, David West, a big, laconic, gracious man who is a Lieutenant in the Georgia State Patrol by day, grills the steaks out back by night. They recommend (for $5.50 complete) a New York sirloin strip that would make the cliff dwellers in Manhattan juicy with howling envy if they knew about it. They also have fine T-bones, and a rib-eye priced at $3.25. The Secret Service agents assigned to Jimmy often eat

there, as do the men and women of the national press when this President-in-waiting pulls them, in his wake, into town. As a matter of fact, the word is out that persons in Plains, Persons Deserving of Respect, have suggested that Faye and David dismantle their operation and move it one mile south and nine miles west, where a fine restaurant is about the only thing that the people of Plains want that they don't already have.

Early July in Plains, Georgia, is hot summer and the prevailing sky seems to be filled with heavy cloud reluctant to disburden itself of rain. What is unexpected, as you ride west on U.S. 280 through the evening countryside, is the wondrous majesty of huge cumulus formations riding under a canopy of soft yet somewhat steely blue. Suddenly looming ahead of you is not what you remember from photos you've seen—not the familiar small row of vintage 1925 storefronts—but a large, handsome water tower cylinder straight out of the modern age. As you drift in toward town, you find Neal's sandwich shop on the right; on the left, drums of Carter's Liquid Fertilizer, along with crop-drying machines, sheds, warehouses and unfamiliar odd buildings all apparently associated with the business of agriculture. Then you see the Williams Service station on your right and the one-story Carter's Warehouse office on your left. The Williamses, whose own peanut processing and warehouse operation is up the street, are "the other company" in town. In fact, the short way of describing the economy of Plains is to say that the Carters own half and the Williamses own the other half. But it is not really so. And there was a time, not terribly long ago, when no Carters owned anything at all in Plains, Georgia.

If you've never been "down home," when you come into Plains, Georgia, you immediately discover what it's supposed to be like. You see that row of neat storefronts, now tidied up, on Main Street, alongside railroad tracks which long ago belonged to the SAM Railway—the Savannah, Americus & Montgomery—and now constitute a rarely used track of the Seaboard Coast Line. If you want Main Street in all its quietude, a good time for a second visit is on a late July evening. Just before dusk this particular evening, the stranger encountered an astonishing sunset, which painted the frame buildings in an unearthly rose-colored aura. There are those among the local populace that think Jimmy was divinely sent down from some mountain to save America from the wreck of Watergate and from Republican and other ruination. Tonight the sunset fire lights not only Main Street but the entire town with its soft red glow.

But when you return next morning, the town is all bustle; at the end of Main Street, Carter's Antiques and Country Store is open for business. Hugh Carter, a freckle-faced, sandy-haired, fifty-five-year-old first cousin of Jimmy's—who in 1966 succeeded to Jimmy's Senate seat in the Georgia State Assembly in Atlanta—is the owner. But his eighty-seven-year-old father, Alton Carter, brother of the late "Mister Earl," Jimmy's father, is there, truckin' hard, helping Hugh. Mister Alton, the first of the Carters to move into Plains to set up in business there, is the man who raised Earl from the time he was a small boy. He is the Carter family member in Plains with the longest recollection, and will gladly tell you about the local ancestors and how they came to this part of Georgia. Mr. Alton comes on as a man of stern visage whose face shows his identification with the Carter trait he calls "good hard common sense." But as you talk to him about the family, he will break now and then into a smile and a wink, and in the end will likely be grinning broadly as he offers a privileged visitor a bottle of his homemade apple wine. He can legally make two hundred gallons a year of this and cucumber and tomato and wild grape and other wine, and though he says he has yet to take his first drink, you must assume from his enthusiasm for the wine and its making that Mr. Alton's teetotalism does not disinclude an occasional snootful of this vinous brew, which must be the most sinfully tasty apple thing that has happened to mankind since Adam took that first bite in the Garden of Eden, thereby launching the human race on its career of wickedness and hard work.

The great-great-granddaddy of them all—the local Carters—is, according to Mr. Alton, a man named Wiley Carter who, in 1840, settled in Schley County up above Sumter County, at a place about eleven miles from Plains. This local progenitor is buried in the old Carter cemetery

not far from where he lived and not far from the house of Ann Ansley whom he married.

Wiley Carter came from Warrenton, Georgia, a town between Macon and Augusta. He came over to homestead—several thousand acres, probably. He had twelve children, and after he died left nearly all of them sizable tracts of land. Wiley Carter was, of course, not the first of the Carters to live in the United States. Wiley was himself descended from a James Carter of Virginia who was born in 1737, and fought in the Revolutionary War. In fact, the roots from the American Carter tree run wild: keeping track even of Georgia relatives would be a full-time occupation for any man or woman. And one gets the impression, tracing some of these runners, pegs, sprouts, and tendrils with the help of Mr. Alton, that if all the original Carter descendants or relatives in the United States were to cast their ballots for Jimmy, the Republicans would be unable to raise a quorum, much less a serious national vote. But there seems to be more to the Carter ancestry than even Mr. Alton is able to remember.

After you've poked around among the ancestral bones in Plains and driven with Mr. Alton up to the original Carter cemetery in Schley County, you travel back over to Americus and discover there a kind of mad monk twenty-year-old genealogist, who arrives on the scene complete with a page boy haircut, an Episcopalian reputation and priestly ambitions. He is named R. L. Ranew; his first name is really Ronald. This young man has since the age of twelve been following the galloping Carter roots hither and yon. He's a fifth generation Carter himself and has been stirred to special effort by the exciting spectacle of a Carter presidency.

Now this is when those roots get up on horseback and go roaring off in the direction of legend and myth. South-

erners know all about these weird heraldries. But you may not, and suddenly your mind begins exploding because Ron Ranew has surfaced from his studies with what has to be considered, at least by a near-immigrant Northerner, an awesome hypothesis—that Jimmy Carter comes upon us straight from Alfred the Great, King of England. "Yes, a twenty-ninth generation direct descendant," Ron says, with firmness and enthusiasm. His ultimate authority for all this is a clutch of genealogists of fairly decent reputation in England, people long since passed away—although some of the English part of the research was redone in the late 1950s for a William Carter of Atlanta.

The Alfredic line is traced through to a Captain Thomas Carter who, according to Ron, was the original Carter to set foot in the New World. This Thomas Carter, who was called Sir Thomas by his servants, wasn't actually knighted. But he was enough of a Sir to suit the servants, since he was a captain in the militia, a member of the Virginia House of Burgesses, and a vestryman of Christ Church in Caroline County, Virginia. Born in 1631, he came to America in 1650, died on his own plantation, Bardford, on October 27, 1670. Cap'n Tom, Sir, doesn't sound much like a forefather of Baptists. More a Cavalier than a Puritan, he is remembered as a man who had squandered away most of his father's fortune in London. In the final throes of this squandering, he met and married, on May 4, 1640, Catherine Dale, daughter of a Major Edward Dale. The Dales had intermarried with the very powerful Skipwith family of Northampton and Lincolnshire, and it is through this line that the tie to Alfred the Great is traced.

Through the Skipwiths who had married into the family of Sir Lionel Dymoke, it runs to Sir Lionel Dymoke's grandfather, Sir Lionel de Welles; and from Dymoke and de Welles, the line continues through the Greystokes, the Cliffords, the Berkleys, the La Zouches, the De Quinceys,

the Vermondoises, then through Henry and his father Edward the Elder, King of England, to Alfred himself, the greatest English king, who

> saw wheels break and work run back
> And all things as they were
> And his heart was orbed, like victory,
> And simple, like despair . . .

There is also a line, according to Ron Ranew, running back all the way to the daybreak of French royalty. It traces from the Clifford family, through the Robert Vipount family through John FitzGeoffrey, through Hugh Bigod and Roger Bigod—men who signed the Magna Carta—back to the Plantagenet line of England. Through Hameline Plantagenet it goes to Geoffrey Plantagenet, son of King Henry the First, then through Henry to William the Conqueror to Robert the Magnificent, Duke of Normandy, and then to Richard II and on to Richard the Fearless of France; thence to William Longsword, to Rollo the Dane, First Duke of Normandy, then to Pepin of Valois, King Pepin II, and King Pepin I; then to Bernard, King of Lombardy: thence it goes to Charlemagne, King of the Franks, Ruler of the West, and Holy Roman Emperor.

Whether all these papist antecedents will in the end bring Mr. Carter an endorsement from the God of Rome and the Catholic bishops of America, remains to be seen. But it should be pointed out that through Jimmy's great-great-grandmother, Ann Ansley, there is a direct tracing, for protection perhaps, back to Susannah Annesly, who must have been a good enough originator of Methodists, since she gave birth to John Wesley, who was the first. These variously spelled Annesleys, of Nottinghamshire, England, also gave rise to Sir William Ansley, the first Chief Justice of New Jersey, who surfaced in America in 1769.

Among the less savory of the tribe, according to Ranew, is the Sir Francis Annesley of Mountnorris (County Down, Ireland) the first Viscount Valentia (County Kerry, Ireland), whose dates are 1585 to 1660. Sir Francis was Secretary to James I when the first idea of the infamous Ulster Plantations came up, and was directly responsible for bringing the rabble of Scotland across into Northern Ireland. Putting it mildly, these were mostly "pore Scotch trash"—tenant farmers, criminals, and worse. They are led today, it might be added, by a brutalitarian named Ian Paisley, who has a doctorate of some kind from a certain Southern university, which thereby (God help us all) carries almost alone into the late 1970s the burden of the Shame of the South. At least this can be said: current reports out of Georgia back alleys reveal no one down there who can, for violent old style demagoguery, touch the hem of Paisley's doctoral cloak. For vivid ethnic hatred of the murder-inciting variety these days, it is necessary to go back across the ocean to unhappy Belfast, where the Northern Irish Catholics are the despised and downtrodden racial minority—"niggers" of the Seventies, to Paisley's mean redneck bully boy Prods.

Going up Georgia Highway 49 from Americus, if you drive about the same distance as you would to get to Plains, you come to Andersonville, a town of less than 400 people.

Nearby is the famous National Cemetery. A sign near the entrance says: "Here in mass graves lie the remains of 12,912 prisoners-of-war who died at Andersonville. They were buried in trenches, shoulder-to-shoulder with their comrades. . . . Veterans and servicemen of all later wars now rest alongside the men of the Civil War."

It is a symbol of our complicated sad history— Andersonville—the story of an American death camp situated on a heavily polluted branch of a stream called Sweetwater Creek; the story of a commandant, Captain Henry Wirz, who tried to get food and medical supplies and bedding for a prison population three times too large for this camp, and who was hanged as a war criminal in Washington, D.C., in 1865, the same year the conflict ended; a story of Southern and Northern harshness and brutality and murder; yet unlike the stories of Dachau or Auschwitz or Buchenwald a story also of nobility and decency—perhaps among Confederate troops especially.

Somehow also symbolized by all of this, the visitor realizes, is the South that once was—in truth, in part, a South of meanness and violence, of mobs of the hopelessly poor and ill-educated. Yes, there are people alive in Georgia today who remember how vigilante groups would go looking for "niggers" to lynch on Saturday night. You hear tales, softening with fading recollection now, of dirt-poor whites, living and partly living, coming like savages from their paperboard shacks and gathering to listen to the fomenters who moved from place to place, from county to county, stirring votes for themselves by howling out the aboriginal racial fears pounding in the dark places of the white man's breast.

Yet all but gone now from the memories of the young are images of fiery crosses burned on hillsides by the white-sheeted provokers of the Ku Klux Klan, to the echo of cries for blood: the blood of Jews, the blood of Catholics, the blood of the blacks, the blood of Chinese itinerant laborers—any blood at all to pour upon the necessary fires. Later in time, the speeches of the stump demagogues would serve to provide dark vicarious substitution for the actual killing the law increasingly opposed and prevented.

Yet, it is easy for outsiders to forget—especially when thinking about Georgia—that buried in the past of the Southern American nation is also a history of chivalry and nobility, and that of a height and depth no other region can claim. This is the South of Thomas Jefferson, farmer and scientist and universal man; the South of Charles Carroll of Carrollton, a signer of the Declaration of Independence, and a member of the great original American aristocracy, the Maryland aristocracy, which was Roman Catholic. This is the South of George Washington, who was not piped to the presidency by the airs of racist rhetoric. This was a land warm to philosophy and literature, with a quality of settled culture almost unknown in the northern and western reaches of the tiny, restless, itinerant, and ambitious nation.

In time, on a level between the poor violent people and the old gentry, there arose a different kind of Southern American. These were a decent and hardworking, a quieter and very conscientious folk, whose interest was in the management of farming, and in trade. These people drank little, they lived moderately. They suffered from self-righteousness, it is true, and they listened to the racist demagogues, but they voted for the lesser of evils, and they worked alongside black people in their farm fields, which were sometimes sizable, and in their shops and homes. They knew these blacks, whom they sometimes "owned" and cared for, and sometimes set free. Through the generations they bided their time, waiting for their hour to come. They were a proud people, and as little inclined to self-abasement as to self-indulgence. They provided most of the leadership in the great Civil War, which the Confederacy might have won. Jefferson Davis, the great patrician of Mississippi, spoke both for them and for his own aristocracy when he said that Southerners had fought the war against the North for higher principles. "When the cause was lost, what cause was it?" he wrote in 1884. "Not that of the South only, but the cause of constitutional government, of the supremacy of law, of the natural rights of man."

Present-day Southern politicians are often asked to apologize for the depredations of their fathers and great-great-grandfathers. But not all the progenitors saw their lives as having been dedicated to sinfully evil ends. "It has been said that I should apply to the United States for a pardon," Jefferson Davis said. "But repentance must precede the right of pardon, and I have not repented. Remembering, as I must, all which has been suffered, all which has been lost—disappointed hopes and crushed aspirations—yet I deliberately say, if it were all to do over again, I would again do just as I did in 1861." But before he died, he said to a reporter who came to him for some word or sign: "Tell them—tell the world that I only loved America." In later years a visitor from England came, and went away, and wrote about what he perceived to be the spirit of the Southern United States.

> I shall not travel the tracks of fame
> Where the war was not to the strong;
> Where Lee the last of the heroes came
> With the Men of the South and a flag like a flame,
> And called the land by its lovely name
> In the unforgotten song . . .

In war and peace these farmers and tradesmen and professional people of the South continued to send sons into the military, which they saw as a service, remembering and loving and emulating the temperate Robert E. Lee—the soldier who, studying the battlefield at Fredericksburg, said to someone standing near: "It is well that war is so terrible. Otherwise we should grow too fond of it."

It is the twentieth century now, a time of change. One remembers a photograph of another military cemetery at Marrietta, Georgia, northwest of Atlanta, where a black sergeant stood to the colors in front of his men beside the stones. One thinks, wandering among the graveplots at Andersonville: Here among the dead there is no aristocracy of war or peace or season or place or time. In one newer row of graves we find Southerners who served in World War I or II, most of whom died later on: we find Johnny Williams of Georgia, Joseph Perry of Florida, Jimmy Lee Spivey of Georgia, Charlie Harris of Florida, Willie Crawford of Alabama, Wilson Allen of Mississippi. There are some women buried in this section of the cemetery, relatives of soldiers, sailors or marines. In the original burial grounds, there are many, many graves marked simply

UNKNOWN

U.S.

SOLDIER

and in one row, among all these unknowns, there are headstones for D. B. Wilsey of New York, Francis M. Pickett of Company E of the 30th Illinois Infantry, Augustus Kauffman of New York, Conrad Fisher of Pennsylvania,

William Kruger of Wisconsin, Monroe Teneyck of New Hampshire, W. H. Wells, state unknown; the graves of Jeremiah Kennedy of Pennsylvania, William Norwood of Tennessee, Ambrose Maynard of Pennsylvania, Conrad Ducker of Illinois, "H. G. Escue, Corp'l, Tennessee." So run the headstones at Andersonville.

Driving away from the gravesites, onto and along the road which borders at most points the line of the old stockade, one smells the fresh grass, newly mown, and sees the site of Providence Spring from which arose one day, after a storm, as if by miracle, a source of fresh water. However, ten feet, on the average, from the stockade markers are poles fixing "the deadline": if a Union prisoner crossed this, he was to be shot. There is a marker for the Dead House, too, where the men who died of disease, starvation, of wounds or by killing or suicide were taken prior to burial. Nearly 13,000 men died, of a total fourteen-month population of some 45,000.

Why, after all this, did Southerners continue to go to war? And did all those fathers and mothers who sent their sons to the military academies find the same kind of violent satisfaction, if on a subtler plane, as the fire-drinking rednecks found in the harangues of brutalizing politicians? Then one thinks of the virtues of the great commanders bred out of the South, and of the tradition of Lee, and of the West Point motto, "Duty, Honor, Country," and of how so many of these people actually believed in that stoic motto and enriched it with their belief and sacrifice, and then one is lifted again by the force of this now some way newly conceivable challenge:

> Where have they gone that did delight in honor,
> Abrupt and absolute as an epic ends . . .?

What is it—a hundred years and more since the end of the Civil War? Well, these hardworking people of the Southern middle classes also cultivated through that century the slowly yielding soil; they trucked their produce somehow to market. They opened and ran their shops. They occupied themselves with the building of simple manufactures and of hospitals, and attended to the education of their young and of their black dependents, hoping for a better future. Then—suddenly, as history goes—came rocking change, and out of these people and out of migrants drawn in the meantime to the old land from the North, there rose what is now called the New South.

Shaking free of these strange considerations, the visitor drives out the cemetery gate and passes back into the world as it is. You head back toward Americus on Route 49 from Andersonville. A Lear jet slices in toward Souther Field, where people flying in to see Jimmy Carter often land. Yet something remains of your meditation on the Southern dead. And it occurs to you that maybe in this context, the Carters, especially James Earl Carter, Sr., might be better understood.

The bright idea occurs that one way to get an honest picture of "Mister Earl" is to talk to Miz Lillian. In the national press, Mr. Earl, Jimmy's father, has been called all kinds of things, up to and including a bigot and a racist. But why is it that the townspeople do not remember him that way?

Part of the blame for Earl Carter's unsavory reputation must be laid at Jimmy Carter's own doorstep. Put bluntly, Jimmy gets considerable liberal mileage in his very self-revealing book, WHY NOT THE BEST? out of a couple of reconstructed confrontations with his father on the race issue. Was this a dispute, simply, between a father of one generation and a son of another? Kids tend to push their parents ideologically, sometimes not understanding things about custom and habitual attitudes and such. Further to this theory, Jimmy has often said that people in the South cannot be moved by politicians who approach the Southerner with a pompous attitude, who say in effect: I am better than you, and therefore you will have to do thus and so from now on. Did Jimmy learn that lesson from his own experiences with his father?

Anyhow, Miz Lillian is a woman whose progressive spirit excites even Jane Fonda. And Lillian Carter is the kind of woman who could go to India as a Peace Corps volunteer (in 1968) at the age of seventy, and for two years

work among the poor there, ministering with her hands even to lepers. She is Jimmy's mother, and has been for years a sign of hope to liberal journalists looking for something to really love in Jimmy. Miz Lillian is also Earl Carter's widow.

In her town house in Plains, and in her pond house some three miles from Plains, she will talk at length about her husband, who she says was a great smiler like her son, Jimmy—and even more like her rotund son, Billy, who Jimmy says reminds him of his father.

Miz Lillian builds a nest for herself in the deep pillows of her couch. "Earl Carter," she says, "was a man of great integrity. He was considered the best businessman in Sumter County—and the most honest." According to Miz Lillian, Earl was the best friend the farmers had in the county. A man would come to Earl for seed or feed or other essentials. Or the man would come for help in buying a farm or for a mortgage on the farm, and Earl would provide what was needed. (According to his brother Alton, who says that Earl was a far better businessman than he, there were six hundred or so farmers in the area, most of whom came to Earl Carter for help at one time or another. Earl was careful whom he lent money to, Alton says, so he rarely had any occasion to foreclose.)

Before Earl died—he knew he was going to die of cancer—he had an operation. Five days after the operation he was brought home because he had some business that needed attention. He asked Jimmy, who had come back from the Navy to see his dying father, to bring home the books of accounts. In the case of half a dozen farmers, Earl decided at his death to have Jimmy cancel the notes for the money they owed, because he knew they would be unable to pay up.

"When Earl died," Miz Lillian says, "Jimmy saw grown men crying. That's the kind of man Earl was."

As a young woman, Lillian Gordy had come over to Plains from her native Richland, Georgia, to learn to be a nurse. It was a Dr. Sam Wise who directed her training. Wise was a member of a family of doctors famous all over the area. Lillian Gordy had been dating a boy named George Tanner. Dr. Sam took her aside one day, and said, "I don't like you going out with him. I'll tell you who I would like you to go with. It's Earl Carter. He's a boy that has more ambition than anybody in this town, and he's going to be worth a lot some day." Lillian at first didn't like Earl, because she didn't like the girl he had been going with. But eventually she fell in love with him. Why this change of heart? "He was just so sweet to me."

They had different dating customs back then, Lillian says. "You didn't kiss a boy in those days. If people saw you kissing a boy, you were considered very wild." Lillian admits that she kissed Earl before they were engaged. "But nobody knew it. I didn't let anybody see me. And I dated

him at least two months before I let him kiss me." They did hold hands during the two months. "But that's about all, I'm telling you!" And of course people didn't sleep together until they were married. "Oh. No, no, no!" On their first date Earl and Lillian went to Americus and saw a play—THE MERCHANT OF VENICE. Lillian says, "It cost five dollars a seat, and we felt just terrible." When she saw that it was going to cost five dollars, she said she didn't want to go. Earl said, "Well, we're going. We're already here." Lillian reflected that there was no place to sit on a date in those days. "So we saw the play. It was a beautiful play and I enjoyed it—especially Portia." All through their lives together, she says, they laughed about it—paying that much money to see a play.

After that first time, when they went out together, they used to go riding. "When it was time for us to do our courting, Earl had bought a farm, and we would take a ride out to the farm." There were two years of courting in all, and one year of engagement. They married in 1923, as soon as Lillian had finished her training. Earl had planted a lot of Irish potatoes. "We were going to have our honeymoon from the sale of the potatoes." They postponed their honeymoon. "As I recall, the potatoes didn't do so well."

Jimmy was born in 1924, a year and three days after they were married. Next came Gloria, and then Ruth. Billy was not born until 1937, thirteen years after Jimmy. "All of my children," says Lillian, "worshiped their daddy. They loved Earl better than they did me." In a way? "Well, yes, in a way." The family ritual at night involved the children coming to their father when they were small. "They would come in, lean against Earl's shoulder—if we were playing bridge, for instance—and would say their prayers to Earl.

> Now I lay me down to sleep,
> I pray the Lord my soul to keep.
> If I should die before I wake
> I pray the Lord my soul to take.

And then Jimmy would say, 'God bless Mother, Daddy, Gloria, Ruth—and, later, Billy—and make me a good boy, Amen.' And after they would say it, Earl would kiss them goodnight and they would kiss me, and that was it. Earl was the best father on earth."

You can, you discover, ask Lillian any question. "I might not answer it. But you can ask me. Go ahead." Okay: Was Earl a racist or bigot? Miz Lillian does not seem disturbed by the question; she is in fact energetic in answering it. "You must understand that we didn't discuss these things at home. In those days there was no such thing as integration or segregation. Association with black people was an everyday thing." There were only two white families out there in Archery. The rest were black. Lillian, a trained nurse, looked after the black people on their farm whenever they were ill. "I went to them and I doctored them, you might say. Because they were poor. This was a long, long time ago." She took them medicines. She went up to see what was wrong. "If I didn't know what to do, I would call Dr. Sam Wise and he would tell me what to do. We had an understanding that if anybody was too poor to have a doctor even for surgery, Dr. Sam would do it if I would nurse them through the worst of the sickness. We did that for years and years. My husband did all of the financial part of it. He paid for what was needed. Earl was willing to do this, and he wanted to do it, and I never heard him speak an unkind word about the black people. At one time we had about 250 Negroes living on our farm. In those days you weren't buddy-buddy with them. But it wasn't segregation, and it wasn't integration. It was the custom of the South."

Did Earl see Lillian as pushing back the horizons for Southern whites? "I think he did. You must understand that we didn't discuss these things. Yet I knew that Earl was

very proud of me." Miz Lillian settles deeper into her couch. "You know, a man from a magazine in New York came to see me, and said when he entered the house, 'I want to tell you, Mrs. Carter, that there's hardly a black man of culture in the United States who doesn't know about you, and what you've done.' All right, that's the way it's been. But as liberal as I am—and everybody knows it!—if Earl had lived—he's been dead now twenty-four years—I believe that he would feel exactly as I do." In all her care and concern for the blacks, Miz Lillian said, her husband was aware of what she was doing and approved it and stood by it. "He was kind, he was a gentleman to everybody, black and white."

If James Earl Carter, Sr., was, in the eyes of his wife Lillian, a man of integrity, who gave her in her activism proud if silent support, and "the best father any children ever had," well, Lillian Carter is herself nearly everyone's heroine. Hunter S. Thompson, in his hilarious ROLLING STONE piece, "Jimmy Carter and the Great Leap of Faith: An Endorsement with Fear and Loathing," says: "His seventy-eight-year-old mother, Miss Lillian . . . is the only member of the Carter family I could comfortably endorse for the presidency . . . with no reservations at all." The Northern liberal's Southern liberal par excellence, she is the darling of the media. A lot of people feel she makes the most brilliant prospective American Queen Mother (her strengths are different from those of Rose Kennedy) since Year One of the Republic. An extraordinarily gracious and complex woman, she is also generous with criticism of persons and institutions whose behavior she doesn't like.

Get this: The visitor is standing there when the highly competent secretary of a Southern Senator turns up at the Plains railroad depot one day. Lillian, as often, is acting as the receptionist. (Imagine! Imagine yourself walking into the local Carter headquarters down there, and getting a nod personally all your own, and then a cordial Southern welcome, from the blazing bright eyes of the mother of the Next President of the United States of America!) Okay. In walks this lady, and Lillian greets her, herself, as though she were a long lost sister. But then! Then comes a drumfire of questions aimed at reminding the lady that her Senator Boss had not supported Jimmy. "I know that he wanted to help, and contribute to Jimmy's campaign," says Miz Lillian. "He wanted to help, but he didn't. Probably just wasn't in the mood." The word "mood" hangs in the air. The secretary lady is speechless. And if not at that very minute, then all that night you know she is going to revolve the question in her soul: Why didn't she get her Senator Boss behind Jimmy Carter before it was too late? It was now too late.

But always the criticism is softened by Miz Lillian's marvelous voice, and by a saving note of modesty. She is immensely intelligent, a kind hostess and a national reservoir of courtesy and subtle wit. The reason she will also henceforth be a national monument is that she is in herself the explanation for at least one-half of Jimmy's political sense. Canny old Alton Carter, Lillian's brother-in-law, says: "Lillian? I'll tell you what you'll find out about her. She's a real politician. That's where Jimmy's political instinct comes from. It wasn't from any of the Carters. Her daddy was Jim Jack Gordy, postmaster in Richland, west of here. He was interested in every election that ever came up. If you were a local man, and wanted to be elected, all you had to do was to get him behind you."

He was a big man, Jim Jack Gordy, about six feet tall, weighed about a hundred and ninety pounds. "The Carter side had this good hard sense," Alton says. "They didn't delve into politics too much. It was the Gordys that got Earl into state politics in later life. He was a state representative for about a year before he died. Both families were good folks. But it was the Gordys that had their head in politics."

Over in Richland, people still remember zest as the hallmark of the Gordys. Especially Lillian's father: "Lordy, Lordy, Jim Jack Gordy!" they used to say. Well the father had this daughter, and the daughter had this son. So it goes.

Not surprising—to find out that Jimmy, as a small child, learned to pray, learned to read, and learned to work. There were the night prayers. Then at meals the Carters would have a blessing. And it would be Earl, as the man of the household, who would ask it. "He would sit at the head of the table, all would bow their heads and close their eyes, and he would say, 'Lord, make us thankful for these and many other blessings. Amen.' That was it," Lillian says, "and that was all."

"Jimmy's Mama," as she signs herself in autographs, viewed prayer, then as now, very practically. She doesn't expect that every prayer will be answered. A prayer, for example, "Oh Lord, don't let it rain," is not a prayer that she would expect to have answered. "But every prayer that I actually mean is answered. If I pray, and I pray diligently, my prayers are answered. I have a great thing on prayers being answered."

Nobody who knew Jimmy when he was a young boy remembers his getting into many fights, although he does tell a story of shooting Gloria in the rear with a BB gun once when she had thrown a wrench at him. When his father came home, Jimmy was given a whipping. But he was a quiet lad, and even apparently a kind of peacemaker, and he spent a great deal of his time reading. He read beyond his years, and became a great reader, like his mother. He would read at breakfast, at lunch, and at supper. This habit persisted into later life. His friend John Pope remembers that, later, when Jimmy was a young businessman, he would often read right through lunchtime.

He came early to the discipline of hard work. As Jimmy describes some of this, he sounds a little like an agrarian Tom Sawyer. He had to paint his own fences, of course, and he had dark-skinned contemporaries. His work was generally done alongside black boys of his own age. But it was not a city boy's work. "We ground sugar cane, plowed mules, pruned watermelons, dug and bedded sweet potatoes, mopped cotton [a task Jimmy grew to hate], stacked peanuts, cut stovewood, pumped water, fixed fences, fed chickens, picked velvet beans, and hauled cotton to the gin together." There was also plenty of time, he says, for country sports of various kinds: "We hunted, we fished, explored . . . we also found time to spend the nights on the banks of Chocktawhatchee and the Kinchafoonee Creeks, catching and cooking catfish and eels when the water was rising from heavy rains. We ran, swam, rode horses, drove wagons and floated on rafts"—he and the little black children together. "We misbehaved together and shared the same punishments. We built and lived in the same treehouses and played cards and ate at the same

44

table." As Jimmy grew up, he learned to read more. As a boy, encouraged by his mother, by Miss Julia Coleman and other teachers, he read widely, by his own account, in literature; and he learned about religion, art and music.

When Jimmy was still in grammar school, he conceived the notion—probably instilled in him by postcards sent from far ports by his sailor uncle, Tom Gordy—of going to the Naval Academy at Annapolis. His father encouraged him. Jimmy was not yet in his teens when he first wrote to find out what the admission requirements were.

An early graduate of Plains High School—at sixteen years of age—he went on to attend Georgia Southwestern College in Americus for a year, then went on to Georgia Tech to get courses he needed before entering the Naval Academy. He spent two semesters in ROTC there. One reason he did so well later at Annapolis, graduating in the top eight percent of his class, was his preparation in math and science at Tech.

When he graduated from Annapolis, he went back to Plains and married Rosalynn Smith, then a student at Georgia Southwestern. She was three years younger than he, and had been a close friend of Jimmy's younger sister Ruth. Rosalynn was nineteen, he twenty-two. His ambition for her growth, and her love for him, conspired to turn her into a superb political professional, a more effective campaigner perhaps than any wife in the history of presidential politics. The Rosalynn Smith whom Jimmy Carter married was shy and quiet in the extreme. But they say she always had that incredibly charming smile.

Jimmy applied for submarine duty and eventually qualified as a submarine commander. He was never senior enough, while in the Navy, to have a ship of his own. Later he qualified as a member of Admiral Hyman Rickover's team, working on the development of the first atomic submarines. He taught crew members mathematics, physics, and atomic technology. He took graduate courses in reactor technology and nuclear physics at Union College in Schenectady, New York, and applied what he had learned in helping develop a prototype power plant. He conceived a great admiration for the demanding Rickover, whom he describes as "probably the most competent and innovative naval engineer of all time." He says that the Admiral had a profound effect in shaping his life, comparable to that of Lillian and Earl. He also says: "We feared and respected him and strove to please him." According to Jimmy, Rickover probably knew more about the capabilities of the manufacturers who supplied the components of atomic submarines than the manufacturers themselves knew. But perhaps the most significant thing about his submarine experience is that Jimmy Carter became expert in all kinds of technical areas. It has been said of him that he knows more than anyone else in public life about nuclear technology—and weaponry.

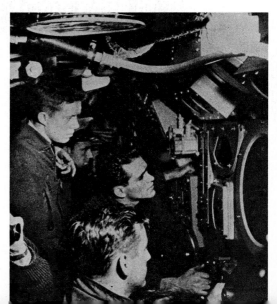

Jimmy Carter gives the circumstances of his departure from the Navy and his return to Plains: "I worked for Rickover until 1953, when my father died of cancer. I was permitted to go home on leave during his terminal illness, and I spent hours by his bedside. We talked about old times together and about those intervening eleven years when we had rarely seen each other . . . Hundreds of people came by to speak to Daddy, or to bring him a choice morsel of food or some fresh flowers. It was obvious that he meant much to them, and it caused me to compare my life perspective with his. After his funeral, I went back to Schenectady . . . I began to think about the relative significance of his life and mine. He was an integral part of the community, and had a wide range of varied but interrelated interests and responsibilities. He was his own boss, and his life was stabilized by the slow and evolutionary changes in the local societal structure . . . After some tortuous days, I decided to resign from the Navy and to come home to Plains—to a tiny town, a church, a farm, and uncertain income. . . ."

Lillian adds that the business needed Jimmy. Some $90,000 was owed the family at Earl's death—beyond those half dozen debts Earl had ordered Jimmy to cancel— and it would have to be a family member who would collect the money. The family was well fixed in terms of property, and Earl had left a considerable amount of money to be divided among his wife and children. But there was a good family business, and somebody was needed to run it. Billy, at sixteen was too young for these responsibilities. So, despite the protestations of Rosalynn—who loved their Navy life and saw a great future for him in it—Jimmy Carter came home to Plains.

Poking around and asking questions, you get the impression that as a young businessman Jimmy Carter was not only a peanut farmer and handler, but that some of the experimentation done to improve peanuts as a crop— especially seed peanuts—came to revolve around him and his ability to breed a better goober. He perfected machinery, designing a warehouse his brother Billy says was later imitated all over the country. From the time of Earl Carter's death until Billy took over the business in the early seventies, Jimmy increased annual sales to a level of $800,000 a year.

But you also discover that managing and building the family business didn't take all Jimmy's time. Almost immediately he was elected to the presidency of various civic groups in Plains and in Sumter County. One of his first projects in Plains was to get a swimming pool built, under the sponsorship of the local Lions Club. A small amount of money had been raised, but the pool was built mostly with donated labor. Jimmy's friend, John Pope of Americus, Georgia, was then in the cement business. "He wanted me to help him," Pope says, "on construction of the pool, which was to be a recreation area for the town. He recruited farmers who lived near Plains to come in and help with their tractors and small dirtpans. They dug this large hole—35 by 75 feet—and furnished their own tractors, and their gasoline or fuel oil. The project took a lot of hand labor, mainly in cleaning out the corners. Once the hole had been dug, Jimmy recruited carpenters, along with the local plumber, P. J. Wise. The carpenters built the forms for the pool. We had no ready-mix concrete company in the county, so I took my large cement mixer and a couple of skilled cement finishers and put them to work."

The pool that Jimmy built is still there today: a huge homemade oblong of no great aesthetic appeal. It is, however, very much a functioning community center, and in hot weather it is full of people, youngsters especially—

serving, so it appears, precisely the purpose intended when it was built in 1954.

John Pope and his late wife Marjorie became very close to Rosalynn and Jimmy during this time. He and Jimmy ate lunch at the Carter house. While Jimmy was working on the swimming pool project Rosalynn ran the office almost single-handedly most of the day.

Jimmy and Rosalynn were not socially inactive during these years. They and their friends—people like the Popes, and Billy and Irene Horne of Americus—took a lively interest in the intricacies of square-dancing, and in the waltz (which his friends say Jimmy really liked), the jitterbug, and the rhumba. (Here Jimmy was his father's son. Earl Carter loved to go dancing, and sometimes, when Miz Lillian wasn't in the mood, Earl would take his daughter Ruth out dancing.) They made a study of various kinds of square-dance techniques, and even found their own square-dance caller. Mr. Pope says, "If you lived in Americus or Plains, you had to find something to do. You had to create your own entertainment." They would go out often, especially on weekends, dining together. Since no one in the group was much on drinking, they were constantly on the dance floor. The Carters also played bridge with their friends. They held cookouts in one another's yards. They sometimes went off to Florida vacationing and camping together. As the younger Carter children grew older, they were included in vacation plans.

They were small town Americans—strong on self-improvement. They got together—Jimmy and Rosalynn, John and Marjorie Pope and the Hornes—and took a speed-reading course with a larger group of people. After a time, Jimmy got so far ahead of the group that he was given private lessons by the teacher. Jimmy increased his speed from five hundred words per minute, when he began, to two thousand words per minute at the conclusion of the course, with almost total comprehension. As before, say his friends, anything that Jimmy Carter put his mind to, he was determined to do as well as he could.

During Jimmy Carter's years as a businessman in Plains, Georgia—long before the notion of becoming President entered his head—he began to take positions somewhat more liberal than those of other South Georgians. His mother's attitudes, his years as a student at the Naval Academy and as a naval officer based in the northeast United States and abroad—and his reading as well—had shown him that racial change was coming. Though he could not by argument or example convince his father to adopt new views, he himself had begun to.

Not too long after he returned to Plains—during the early Eisenhower era—the White Citizens' movement found its way into the small town. Two of Plains' leading citizens asked Jimmy to join. One was the chief of police. The other was a Baptist preacher who was also the local railroad agent. Jimmy refused. After much discussion, the men left, reappearing in a couple of days to tell Jimmy that every other white male citizen in the community had joined the council. Again Jimmy refused. A few days later the two men returned, this time with several of Jimmy's close friends—some of them customers of the Carter seed and fertilizer business. If he did not join, the group told Jimmy, his refusal would damage his reputation as a businessman. He had a hard year that first year, they knew—a bad crop left him a profit of only $184. Did he need the five dollars for dues? They offered to pay it for him.

Jimmy told them in no uncertain terms that his refusal was final. In one version he is supposed to have told them that before he'd give them five dollars, he would flush it down the toilet. He would not become a member under any circumstances. If necessary he would leave the town of Plains, he said. The result was a boycott organized against his business—but it lasted only a short time.

As a member of the Sumter county school board, and later its chairman, Jimmy came under attack for policies seen by fellow whites as unduly supportive of black education. And a confrontation in his church again brought him into conflict with his neighbors in Plains. It was in the early Sixties, now, when black civil rights activists were organizing pray-ins in white churches throughout the South. In

Carter's Baptist church in Plains, where Jimmy was one of the twelve deacons, blacks had historically been invited to attend important events, but for many years it had not been the custom for them to attend regular services. There was an important deacons' meeting Jimmy missed, at which the pastor and the eleven other deacons voted unanimously to oppose the entry of any blacks coming to attend regular church services. The vote upset Jimmy.

His friend John Pope recalls what happend next. The Popes and the Carters had planned a weekend in Atlanta. It seems there was a wedding to attend; but they would also be going to the zoo with the children, and to a show and dinner. Jimmy and Rosalynn and the three Carter boys had gone ahead on Friday to do some shopping for school clothes.

"I couldn't get away from work on Friday," John remembers, "so my wife and I were going up on Saturday. Halfway to Atlanta, in the town of Thomastown, I stopped at a gas station and saw Jimmy's car pulling in from the other direction. I was surprised, because I thought he was in Atlanta waiting for us to arrive. He told me that he was very sorry but our weekend was off—he had to go back home. I asked whether someone was sick. He said that nobody was sick, but that when he called home on Friday night his mother Lillian had told him that they were going to have a vote of all church members Sunday on admitting blacks to services."

John admits that he told Jimmy, " 'I don't think you should go home. You're away from home, and everybody knows you're away. This is an easy way to not involve yourself. It wouldn't be healthy for your public image to get involved right now.'

"Jimmy very bluntly told me," John continues, "that there was no way he could stay away from his church. He said he had to get back and speak his mind on this matter, to try to get the support of the church members for an open door policy. I again strongly advised him against getting involved. He had a good excuse, since he was away, to escape it, to stay out of it. Jimmy assured me that he didn't want to escape—that he wanted to be a part of it."

Jimmy went on back to Plains.

And on Sunday morning he stood up to urge the two hundred people present to reverse the previous decision of the deacons and pastor, and permit free entry of blacks, so long as their motives were peaceful. It was God's house, he said, not theirs. Several others gave opposing arguments— then the vote. Only six members, five of them Carters, voted to open services to blacks. Fifty or so voted against Jimmy. About a hundred forty did not vote. Some of these

told Jimmy afterward that although they agreed with his stand, they did not want to vote openly during the meeting.

By no means was all of Jimmy Carter's effort in the church devoted to racial issues. He taught Sunday school; he helped out in various ways. Friends tell a story about his part in a revival in Plains. Church members were assigned to visit people who were not members, and Jimmy drew a man who was a kind of a backwoods fellow—really country, really poor. Nobody had ever been able to get this man to come to church. Jimmy went to visit him, talking about how Jesus was a carpenter, how he had worked with his hands and lived among poor people. It was poor people, Jimmy said, whom Jesus loved most of all. The two became very good friends, and Jimmy discovered that he was very musical, owned some old fiddles and other musical instruments. Jimmy and Rosalynn invited him and his family to their own home one night. The man brought along his children and his instruments and everybody had a good time. "Jimmy," says one of his friends, "was more thrilled over making the friendship of that man than he would be in making the friendship of an 'important' person. But Jimmy saw that he was a man who needed some bringing out, and he enjoyed bringing him out." It is not clear that the man ever actually came to church.

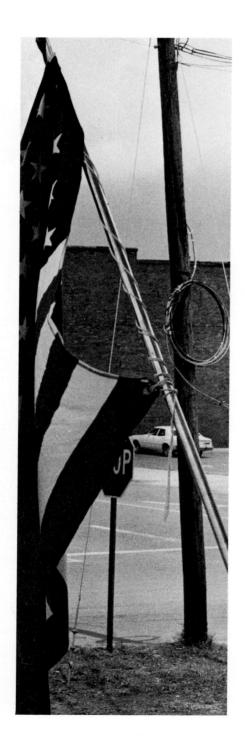

When Jimmy ran for the Georgia State Senate in 1962, his friendship with John Pope stood him in good stead. A certain Joe Hurst was promoting an opposition candidate named Homer Moore—a good enough man, apparently, who was supported also by Sam Singer of Lumpkin, Georgia. The day of the election John Pope, whom Jimmy had asked to be his poll-watcher in Quitman County, witnessed and was later able to recall in precise detail a series of astonishing efforts on the part of Joe Hurst to fix the balloting in Quitman County in favor of Homer Moore. Joe Hurst, who was local political boss in Quitman County, liked to vote dead people, people in federal or state penitentiaries, and people who had moved away to other parts of the state or country. Joe Hurst had come up the hard way, beginning as the owner of a strip of sex spots along a highway between Eufaula, Alabama, and Georgetown, Georgia, and was now a bootlegger. The story goes that Sam Singer pleaded with Joe Hurst not to cheat in this election. Mr. Singer said that Carter could be beaten by Homer Moore without ballot stuffing and other illegalities. But Joe Hurst seems to have been the kind of politico who had an image to maintain. He could not bring himself to break old habits of years' standing—could not resist running the local voting his way. This meant election fraud, and worse. John Pope recounts one of many incidents involving Hurst.

> People in Quitman County were afraid of Joe Hurst—afraid that he would do physical harm to them: burn their house down, or burn their barn down. That day I heard and saw him make this threat. I was at the polls, standing in the voting area at the courthouse in Georgetown, Quitman County, on the date of the senatorial primary. In came a Mr. and Mrs. Spear, who lived in Georgetown and worked in the city of Eufaula, Alabama, across the state line, where they had a small shoe repair shop. Joe Hurst met them at the front door and escorted them into the Ordinary's office, where the voting was done. Collapsible voting booths were available, but during this particular election, they didn't even set them up; the voting was across an open desk.

> The Spears, who were in their seventies, took their ballots and walked down the hall to get away from Joe. They placed the ballots up against the wall and voted their candidates. Thinking to prevent Joe from seeing how they voted, they both folded their ballots several times, ending with a very small knot of paper. They put their hands down into the ballot box—made of cardboard with a hole of five inches or so in the top—scattering their ballots among the other ballots to hide them.

> When they started to leave the courthouse, Joe

Hurst said, "Wait a minute, Mr. Spear! Let me see if you've learned how to vote. You know I've been trying to teach you for a long time." Then Hurst ran his hand into the ballot box and easily found both ballots, since they'd been folded differently from the others. He pulled them out, opened both of them up, and said, "Now I see that neither one of you has learned how to vote yet. Let me teach you, just one more time." Then Joe proceeded, before their eyes, to tear up the two ballots that the Spears had placed in the box. Joe said to the Ordinary, who was Doc Hammond, "Doc, give me some ballots, so that I can teach them." So Doc Hammond tore off six ballots and gave them to Joe Hurst. Joe voted each ballot, scratching out Jimmy Carter's name and leaving Homer Moore's, and folded them all into one package—all six ballots—and placed them in the ballot box. Then Joe said, "Now, Mr. and Miz Spear, that's how you're supposed to vote—the way I tell you. If I ever catch you voting wrong again, I'll burn your house down." All this was done while I and several other witnesses watched.

That was the true Joe Hurst—he was afraid of no one, and spoke very freely of how he ran Quitman County. So I said, "Joe, don't you know you're not going to get away with this? Don't you know that I'm here to see that there's going to be a hereafter?" Joe Hurst said, "I've been running my county for twenty-seven years, and this is the way I run it, and nobody from Sumter County is going to dictate what I will do. And I'd just like for you to know, Mr. Pope, that I put three men in that river for doing less than you're doing here today." I took this as something of a real threat, but didn't worry about it. I intended to stay very public and out in the open. I had no intention of getting off by myself, because Joe Hurst did have a large group of followers, involved in his bootleg business, and they ruled with a strong iron hand . . .

Jimmy Carter lost that election by a few votes, but John Pope kept his promise to Joe Hurst. John's evidence did eventually help provide a "hereafter"—with the aid of Warren Fortson and Charles Kirbo, who acted as Mr. Carter's attorneys in the case. After months of touch-and-go, seesaw effort, and decisions and reversals running right up to the eve itself of the general election, the Homer Moore victory was finally thrown out, and a by now exhausted Jimmy Carter was declared the nominee. He was elected State Senator by a margin of about 1500 votes.

Thus, Jimmy Carter learned very early on some hard lessons in politics. He says that one of the great things he learned was that there were people like John Pope, Warren Fortson, and Charles Kirbo who could be counted on in

difficulty. Joe Hurst eventually went to jail—for bootleg-
ging. Two years later a new Election Code was passed by
the General Assembly, in Jimmy Carter's first senatorial
term. During the debate, someone, Jimmy writes,
"suggested as a compromise that no one be allowed to vote
who had been dead more than three years."

As a Georgia State Senator Jimmy Carter worked hard.
Not even his enemies denied this. He even fulfilled a somewhat foolish campaign promise to read every bill that went
through the legislature. It was useful, in that Jimmy could
prove to the voters that he was willing, as ever, to put forth
more sheer effort than anyone else they could vote for. What
made it somewhat foolhardy is that plenty of those bills
would not have been worth reading. Jimmy is rueful about
having made the promise, and then having had to keep it.
But he did keep it. And he also set out to familiarize himself
with every facet of state government. A fellow legislator
recalls that Jimmy would sometimes stay up all night
studying, and the next day would go over and talk to a
department head to find out how that department
functioned. He had a lot of resilience. A friend from that era
remembers him walking to the Capitol each morning the
legislature was in session. When he could, Jimmy stayed at
the old Piedmont Hotel, which, with its polished brass
doorknobs and other appurtenances bespoke an earlier,
courtlier age. Jimmy was considered by some a good if
sometimes difficult legislator; and there is something about
him having been selected an outstanding Senator by his
colleagues. But he bridled at the old boy-system when it
stood in his way. A segregationist named Peter Zack Geer
was Lieutenant Governor at the time, and therefore presid-
ing officer of the Senate. Geer had a friends' list, and if you
weren't on the friends' list, Geer could make difficulties for

you. Jimmy never made any effort to get on that list, but he did apparently win a grudging admiration from Geer and others for his sincerity and hard work, especially in the area of education.

Some of that work was, however, applied in directions counter to the views prevailing among his constituents, if not necessarily counter to their best interests. Jimmy Carter opens up a window for us on his feelings and his fears while a member of the Georgia Senate, with this remarkable reminiscence of that time:

"The first speech I ever made in the Georgia Senate, representing the most conservative district in Georgia, was concerning the abolition of thirty questions that we had so proudly evolved as a subterfuge to keep black citizens from voting and which we used with a great deal of smirking and pride for decades or generations ever since the War between the States—questions that nobody could answer in this room, but which were applied to every black citizen that came to the Sumter County Courthouse or Webster County Courthouse and said, 'I want to vote.' I spoke in that chamber, fearful of the news media reporting it back home, but overwhelmed with a commitment to the abolition of that artificial barrier to the rights of an American citizen. I remember the thing that I used in my speech, that a black pencil salesman on the outer door of the Sumter County Courthouse could make a better judgment about who ought to be sheriff than two highly educated professors at Georgia Southwestern College."

In 1966, Jimmy went through a very difficult first race for the governorship. He had little money or political organization—just himself, aided and abetted by Rosalynn and Miz Lillian and others among their family and friends. He toured the state seeking votes. But he failed, running third in the Democratic primary, which was won—as was the general election—by one Lester Maddox. It was Jimmy's first and last loss in running for high public office. The next time he took aim at the governorship, Jimmy Carter would be much better prepared.

Losing was hard. Not only was he deeply in debt but he entered an untypical and prolonged period of depression, and lost twenty-two pounds.

What are the roots that clutch, what branches
    grow
Out of this stony rubbish? Son of man,
You cannot say, or guess, for you know only
A heap of broken images, where the sun beats . . .

For Jimmy it was a time for questioning his personal values and goals. One day in late 1966 he took a long walk with his sister, Ruth Carter Stapleton, in a pine woods near Plains. Ruth recalls it this way: Jimmy told her, she says, that he noticed something different in her life—an inner peace which he longed for. "I told him my faith was simple and childlike. I shared my experiences with him and told him that Jesus was not someone who lived two thousand years ago, but was real today, with the power to heal and

give peace and serenity. I explained that a born-again Christian is someone who has come to grips with his or her spiritual dimension. With this awareness comes strength, stability, and wholeness of life." Jimmy recalls: "Ruth asked me if I would give up anything for Christ, if I would give up my life and my possessions—everything. I said I would. Then she asked if I would be willing to give up politics. I thought a long time and had to admit that I would not." Ruth warned Jimmy that until he was willing to give up everything for Christ he would be plagued with self-doubt. The result was that Jimmy underwent the religious rebirth experience that has caused him so much difficulty with unbelievers and skeptics among the public, but brought him, by his own account, serenity. He was, he says, "born again." In his own words, "I established a more intimate relationship with Christ. I developed a deeper sense of inner peace."

In the idiom familiar to Christians, the experience of being twice-born relates to the word of Jesus to Nicodemus: "Except a man be born [again] of water and of the Spirit, he cannot enter into the kingdom of God" (John 3:5, KJV). Some Baptists interpret it this way: the first birth or baptism is of water; the second birth or baptism is of the Spirit.

Perfect serenity is something few achieve. All kinds of people find Jimmy Carter's announcement of his serenity distasteful, and his obvious self-confidence objectionable. Some people get especially angry when they listen to him attribute this to his religious experience. They think he's lying, because they don't have religious experiences. Besides, it's easy for him to be serene, now that he is top dog. But Jimmy may have a different kind of problem, entirely. The serenity, it is sometimes forgotten now, came to him when he was a loser. Not all non-believers will know what that means for a believer who is now a winner.

Anyway, it is interesting that most Atlantans do not recall hearing much, during his four years as Governor, about that twice-born religious experience. Religiousness, genuine or otherwise, was not unusual among politicians in that part of the world.

Part 2
Country Jimmy

In which the outsider shuffles through files containing the strange enough story of a peanut breeder's progress to the Georgia governorship, emerging in a few years, before the startled gaze of the populace, with a presidential nomination; all of which leads to the dizzying conclusion that there seems to be now no way defeat can be seized from the jaws of these victories.

ABC NEWS
ALABAMA
MARYLAND
DELEGATE
THE DEMOCRATIC PARTY OF THE UNITED STATES IN CONVENTION
DELEGATE

Any outsider who ambles around chatting with the homefolk is going to discover very soon, even if he has not read Jimmy Carter's book, or got into dusty back issues of major American newspapers, that there is a certain—well—previousness about this Jimmy Carter goin' off and manifestin' himself beyond the limits of decent modest ambition. So! Jimmy Carter has stuck his neck out before. And he's rode off North before, to regions far removed from the sound of the Plains cowbells, far from the gruntin' kine and the whisperin' of the fructifying peanut plant, to places far away from all those drowsy farmer sounds and cockadoodledoos.

It is one thing to represent the homefolk in the State Senate, which means that a man projects himself for awhile from time to time beyond the home counties, diligent representation of which requires at worst only a couple months of legislative sessions a year. Nothing there to seriously interfere with the progress of the business, especially when you can meanwhile rely on a Rosalynn to look after the fields and sheds and machinery and warehouses of primary concern.

But this governorship trip is another thing entirely. Yep. It became clear quite awhile ago that if Jimmy Carter was going to blush, he was not going to blush unseen. He was not going to be content with those useful toils and hoots of moping owl and silent dusty obscurity. There is this previousness to deal with, the story of the first time that he shuffled forth out of Plains and projected himself onto the larger stage.

So it is necessary to poke around those dusty files of recent yore, because the younger man is father, as the saying goes, of the older man. There might be some trap door here, a backstairs way of descent into Jimmy's psyche, which might tell us something about the country boy Jimmy now knocking on the front door of our era.

Well, it is a weird trail of goings-on which led him from Plains to the Governor's Mansion in Atlanta. Makes it seem easy to follow the strange enough trail which leads—in fact, in a much more straight-arrow kind of way—from Plains to the Presidential Palace. Twisting and stumbling along the path of the earlier career, the wandering outsider is perforce ensnared in the thickets of Georgia politics, which means, among other things, the in some ways delightful spectacle of amazing odd craziness and barefoot baboonery amid the Marriottish decadence of urban America in the supposed-to-be better half of the twentieth century. To sample Georgia politics of this not wholly bygone era is an Asiatic kind of experience, not unlike a warp in which, stepping down from a space platform where moon rockets are taking off, you suddenly find yourself aground among the sheepherders of medieval Tibet.

In the late Fifties and Sixties, while in the great world beyond Georgia an end was coming (at last) to the

Eisenhower era, and Smilin' Jack Kennedy arrived loaded with glamah and vigah and purpose and Boston con, things were still prehistoric down here. One of the fossil survivals was an exclusionary policy with regard to what were generally termed "niggahs"—meaning as it turned out, black people: some of them no blacker than their suntanned white folk Yassuh masters. But the main idea then in Georgia was if those black folk stayed in their places, then everything would be just fine.

Now it happened that during this time—while all over the world Camelot was the main event on TV—these Southern black people suddenly roused themselves into the twentieth century. They woke up educated, many of them; and smart, many of them; yet most of them still without a vote or a decent opportunity.

Martin Luther King had spoken for them from the steps of the Lincoln Memorial in Washington. It was the month of August, 1963:

"It would be fatal for the nation to overlook the urgency of the moment and to underestimate the determination of the Negro. This sweltering summer of the Negro's legitimate discontent will not pass until there is an invigorating autumn of freedom and equality . . . we will not be satisfied until justice rolls down like waters and righteousness like a mighty stream . . .

"I say to you today, my friends, that in spite of the difficulties and frustrations of the moment I still have a dream. It is a dream deeply rooted in the American dream.

"I have a dream that one day this nation will rise up and live out the true meaning of its creed: 'We hold these truths to be self-evident: that all men are created equal.'

"I have a dream that one day on the red hills of Georgia the sons of former slaves and the sons of former slaveowners will be able to sit down together at the table of brotherhood . . .

"I have a dream that my four little children will one day live in a nation where they will not be judged by the color of their skin but by the content of their character.

"I have a dream today . . .

"I have a dream that one day 'every valley shall be exalted, every hill and mountain shall be made low, the rough places will be made plain, and the crooked places will be made straight, and the glory of the Lord shall be revealed, and all flesh shall see it together' . . .

"When we let freedom ring, when we let it ring from every village and every hamlet, from every state and every city, we will be able to speed up that day when all of God's children, black men and white men, Jews and Gentiles, Protestants and Catholics, will be able to join hands and sing in the words of the old Negro spiritual, 'Free at last! Free at last! Thank God Almighty, we are free at last!' "

All right. Here is what happened. Once upon a time Martin Luther King had a dream, and Lester Maddox did not share that dream. And—watch this—Jimmy Carter thought and sought to become Governor of the State of Georgia because Jimmy believed he could do something about Martin Luther King's dream; but Jimmy became Governor with the help of Lester Maddox; and as Governor of Georgia, one of Jimmy Carter's few unquestioned accomplishments was being a good Governor for black people: and thereby Lester Maddox and all the other Maddox-minded people who had supported Jimmy in his quest for that governorship were confounded and made angry. But Jimmy prevailed. That is the short form of the story. The long form of the story—it would take months to figure it all out and a book by itself to tell.

The itinerant who would inquire into all this eccentric behavior is further confronted by plain evidence that Lester Maddox, the apostle of the ax handle, was not, in the circumstances, all that bad a Governor on behalf of Georgia's blacks. Now of course Lester had in 1964 stood at the door of his Pickrick restaurant in Atlanta, brandishing a pistol and surrounded by other white men brandishing ax handles, but later—in 1967–71—Lester was a poor people's Governor, and an oddball Governor, but not exactly a racist Governor. It was a funny rather than a cruel time. One tale is told to the effect that abstemious ole Lester, who held an Open House for citizens every couple of weeks, was accosted on the citizens' reception line one time by a lady who was a striptease artist. "We have a lot in common," he told the woman. "Neither of us smokes or drinks." Anyway he was not the idiot Governor the more advanced—and the more commercial—interests in Atlanta at first feared ("You reckon they thought I was a nut?"). Like many a somewhat demagogic type before him, Lester mongreled and barked about blacks, but in the end he did not bite any. So he was not all that bad for them. Of course, he did not do them much good, either. As with the

Nixiefords on the national scene later on, there was next to no forward motion, except in a few departments like prison reform—in a state where most of the convicts, because convicts come mainly from among the poor, were black. Anyway, when Lester, a man of considerable personal charm, left office in 1971, he also left a great deal of good will behind.

Now out onto this very carefully lit stage steps Jimmy Carter, also a country boy, tricked out in the accoutrements of hick redneckery. In 1966, Jimmy had run for Governor as a sort of liberal and lost. This time, in 1970, he ran as a sort of conservative, and won. This could be a very long story, too, but the gist of it is as follows.

First of all, there was then in Jimmy, as there is now, no small quantity of cunning. He was a close observer of the scene, as always, and he had observed that, for Lester Maddox the common man gambit had worked very well. Jimmy says that he admired Harry Truman. He could just as well say that he admired Lester Maddox. (Not now. Oh, no! That's not the point.) One gathers that what Jimmy admires is not Harry Truman's quick, colorful vulgarity— Jimmy is not publicly vulgar—nor Harry Truman's feisty mouthing-off characteristic. It is Harry Truman's very ordinariness that draws him. "A common man . . . an uncommon leader," is the way Jimmy talked about Truman at the convention. Jimmy must have felt then as now that this commonness at least could not be taken away. Jimmy Carter also saw and identified with Truman's fighting spirit. Despite his occasional limpness of gesture (in this a Southern affectation of gentility?) Jimmy Carter knows he is a fighter, and a stubborn fighter, and finds in himself considerable moral courage. Carter also has to like the eagerness of the Missourian. But many of these same qualities of commonness could be found in Lester Maddox, too, right there in Georgia, circa 1970. But what about Jimmy's liberalism? Well, Jimmy, if he hadn't already found out, could have learned, just from watching Lester alone, that liberalism was not a thing to be made too much of if you were running for high office in Georgia.

Here in our story the footing gets treacherous. At the point where Jimmy is maybe wondering what his liberalism is going to do to him in this second try for the governorship, there heaves onto the scene the figure, both amiable and aloof, of Carl Sanders, a kind of country club good ole boy, whose nickname among the Carterites—purely for the purposes of this election, of course—becomes "Cufflinks Carl." Jimmy sees Carl Sanders coming on, and stakes out a position somewhat to Sanders' right. Now ole Carl had been a good and successful and moderately liberal Governor of Georgia back when (1963–67), and was giving it another try. Jimmy Carter and his handlers produced the now-famous "ugly" picture of Jimmy dressed in an old open-necked shirt. No tie, either: "This is yore friend Jimmy Carter." Right off the bloody farm.

Well, it worked. When Carl Sanders, in the middle of his campaign, fired his advertising agency—which had been presenting him more or less as he was—and tried to rusticate his image, the electorate was only temporarily confused. Sanders tried to run as Carl the Galoot: the farm-folksy near-redneck—and on and all about how he loved "them good grits." Georgians found this hilarious, especially when pictures turned up all over the state of Carl Sanders the White Man's Friend, with a black Atlanta basketball player pouring champagne over his head. So the segregationists voted for Jimmy and the blacks voted against Jimmy. Anyway, in a runoff after the primary, Sanders lost and Jimmy won the Democratic nomination for Governor; and in the November election Jimmy soundly defeated Hal Suit, a TV personality who was the Republican nominee.

In the end it was judged to be true what Jimmy is supposed to have said to some of his black friends: "You'll hate my campaign, but you'll love my incumbency." Jimmy Carter had got himself elected, remembering that Georgia was in the South and that the South meant Southern politics, and that Southern politics meant traditionally a very heavy traffic in ordinariness. He had not run a segregationist campaign, but he had let segregationists and anti-integrationists and marginals think he was one of them: maybe a little pointy-headed, but underneath that egghead he could display a red neck. Yep. He was a farmer from South Georgia and did peanuts for a living. And the people could see that this Jimmy, he was running with Lester (who could not succeed himself, and by coincidence was running for Lieutenant Governor on the same ticket). If Jimmy was runnin' on the same ticket as Lester—ole Lester, who could have been born with that ax handle in his mouth, and who had nice things to say about his running mate Jimmy Carter ("He's gonna be captain of the ship!") and with Jimmy lookin' as though he just stepped out of a window display at a men's wear store in Americus, Georgia—well . . . Jimmy had even gone and had himself photographed—only jokin' of course—behind a sign saying, "This is Maddox Country." All the time smilin' that great big thoroughly hick smile.

Then practically the next thing you know Jimmy Carter is up there on inauguration day, and he's just launched about five paragraphs into his inaugural speech as Governor. And his cute new little baby daughter is there with him, and Lester Maddox is a-smilin' and all the conservatives and archconservatives who launched Jimmy Carter onto this platform are a-smilin', as they look up and see Lester, a man who stirs good feelin's in the folk because he kept the nigrah in his place and didn't make too much noise about it. And they're all sittin' enjoyably on the platform, when suddenly this strikin' new forty-six-year-old Governor, after those few paragraphs of introduction, makes the following statement:

"At the end of a long campaign, I believe I know our people as well as anyone. Based on this knowledge of Georgians North and South, rural and urban, liberal and conservative, I say to you quite frankly that the time for racial discrimination is over. Our people have already made this major and difficult decision, but we cannot underestimate the challenge of hundreds of minor decisions yet to be made. Our inherent human charity and our religious beliefs will be taxed to the limit. No poor, rural, weak, or black person should ever have to bear the additional burden of being deprived of the opportunity of an education, a job or simple justice."

And these astonishing sentences come poundin' in against Lester Maddox's eardrums, and they bang hard against some other ears in that audience, too: Is this the man they have capitulated into the Governor's mansion? Well, Lester had a white man's fit, fit to be tied, and some of the folks in the Georgia legislature were fit to be tied also. They had Jimmy standing there, saying these things, and

then coming on later, saying he wants to plan a reorganization of the entire government of Georgia. Well, Lester said in effect, Gentlemen, we have got to fight this Jimmy Carter fellow, and confound his plans, and oppose his desires, until such time as Jimmy has left office and I can again take over.

Later on, Jimmy would add insult to injury by hanging the pictures of three black folk in the Capitol. These are famous black citizens of our state, said Jimmy, and they are going to have their portraits hung. These poor little black children come to visit the Capitol and see pictures of famous Georgians, and all they see are these white folk up there. But worst of all—worse than putting up the pictures of Lucy Laney and Bishop Henry McNeal Turner, nineteenth-century black people—was putting up the picture of Martin Luther King, Jr.

But Jimmy hung those portraits up in the Capitol, and he arranged for Ben Fortson, the Secretary of State and at that time the most eloquent speaker for such affairs, to get up and make a fine speech on behalf of the fine black folk whose pictures were put up in the Capitol, as a symbolic (and somewhat tokenistic) representation of black leadership in Georgia. As Lester Maddox still points out: In effect Jimmy Carter told them he was goin' to be a good redneck, and here once again he proved he was a liah.

Now Jimmy did quite a number of other things as Governor, besides make that inaugural speech and put up pictures of dead black people. During his four years in office he put large numbers of living black people onto gov-

JIMMY CARTER
GOVERNOR

ernmental boards. And he set out not just to govern Georgia but to reorganize the entire machinery of the government. Like all large-scale plans, his plan had bugs, and various claims are made for and against it. But it does seem that many of the bugs got worked out; and in some areas, at least, the reorganization plan was considered a success. He also professionalized law enforcement, and brought in enlightened prison administrators. Jimmy worked on cleaning up the environment, and set up the Georgia Heritage Trust, which provided funds for the state to acquire property of scenic, historical and archeological importance. He guided through a judicial reform plan, which began to unblock overcrowded dockets and speed the slow administration of justice. Most of his appointments to the judiciary were regarded as good ones, and he wouldn't reappoint someone he didn't believe was doing the job. He also worked to strengthen consumer protection laws.

Above all, he conducted a tremendous sweeping campaign to move forward that governmental reorganization plan, to drive it through the General Assembly, where a substantial part of the membership had at first open contempt for the whole thing. But they got more cooperative, and Jimmy learned to be less stubborn, less of a turtle, and to work with the two hundred seventy-five or so legislators. Eventually he got his plan passed.

He did imaginative things, like bringing filmmakers into Georgia. An ad in a trade journal at this time shows Jimmy pictured in a film director's chair. The copy reads: "Governor Jimmy Carter doesn't know an interlock from an internegative. So, what's he doing in the film business? He's an expert at cutting red tape . . . We'll be frank. Jimmy Carter is after your business." This effort made Georgia one of the leading states in film production.

He reorganized the state health department, putting it under the Human Resources Department. Before the com-

86

ing of Carter, some Georgians say, the mental hospital at Milledgeville was a "snake pit." He changed that, and in a program in which his wife Rosalynn was closely involved set up one hundred thirty community centers for the mentally handicapped throughout the state. He developed a law and order task force, a kind of flying squad, to help local police defuse crisis situations. One of his proudest accomplishments, one with great residual symbolic value today, was the institution of zero-based budgeting. This meant that every department had to justify its entire budget down to Dollar One, each fiscal period.

In the reorganization plan, the number of state agencies was cut back from a total of between sixty-five and three hundred, to a mere twenty-two. One of the most convincing arguments for the success of the reorganization is that of Chip Carter, Jimmy's second son. Chip was an unpaid ombudsman while his father was Governor. The job of an ombudsman (the term is Scandinavian) is to cut red tape and solve people's problems by moving solutions through the bureaucracy, much in the manner of the little man in the Japanese movie "Ikiru." Chip says, "I was an ombudsman for seven months before the reorganization plan went into effect, and for six months after it became effective. My phone calls were reduced, after reorganization, from about one hundred fifty to forty-five, for the same period."

You ask Chip what this reorganization plan actually saved the taxpayers of Georgia. And he answers: "A lot of it depends on where you get your figures. Some estimates do not include inflation. One estimate, beginning in the fiscal year Dad took over, ends the day he went out of office in January, before the money from the previous tax year came in. So estimates vary, depending. If you go from fiscal year to fiscal year, the total saving seems to be one hundred sixteen million. Dad's budget for the last year of his administration was ten million dollars less than the year before—including inflation and everything else. There was an automatic jump in costs, but still the budget itself was lower." After his father had been Governor for a year, Chip says, "He came back the second year and asked for fifty million dollars less in appropriations, instead of for more. It was easy for a Governor to ask for more with growth and inflation—that had always been the case. They found it easy to justify asking for more. But Dad asked for less."

Four or five months after Jimmy Carter became Governor of Georgia, he began to get national attention. A large part of the reason was that inaugural speech of his: "I say to you quite frankly that the time for racial discrimination is over." The national press was careful to note that Jimmy had arrived at the governorship by somewhat devious politics. This going national for Jimmy took the form of a cover story featuring him in TIME, on the New South and the governors who represented this New South. There was also an article about him in LIFE.

One of the most extraordinary public events of his administration—in terms of later repercussions—was an off-the-cuff speech he made at the University of Georgia at Athens, on Law Day, May 4, 1974. What was extraordinary about this talk was not the reaction at the time—there doesn't seem to have been much of any—but its effect on one journalist, and through him on American journalism as a whole. Hunter S. Thompson is a far-out, spaced-up journalist, who works for ROLLING STONE when he works, and who became politically famous as the author of a series of articles eventually put into a book titled FEAR AND LOATHING: ON THE CAMPAIGN TRAIL 72. The impression one gets is that Thompson, a self-styled doctor of chemotherapy, subsists mainly on speed, Wild Turkey, and Heineken's. But his writing has a kind of desperate last-gasp mad absolute honesty about it and after he heard the Law Day speech Thompson became not only a Jimmy Carter political convert and friend but also Jimmy's apologist among journalistic liberals in America—many of whom began to regard Thompson with emotions running from dismay to disgust for his sponsorship of Jimmy Carter.

The Law Day address was witnessed by at least one important national political personality—Senator Edward M. Kennedy of Massachusetts, who had been overnighting with Jimmy in connection with his own involvement in the Georgia Law Day ceremonies. Now it is clear that by this time—mid-1974—Jimmy Carter had made up his mind that he was going to run for the presidency of the United States. (More on that wild notion later.) But there is something totally spontaneous and unrehearsed about the Law Day address, and nothing in it indicates that Jimmy Carter

even suspected the talk would go beyond the immediate audience. Clearly it was not a carefully planned and articulated speech, and it is replete with malapropisms and various other clumsy twists of the speechifying tongue. But the talk itself was something else. Not only did Jimmy reveal his heart to the people attending the ceremonies, but because of Dr. Thompson, he reveals it to us. The talk is now, in all its awkwardness, a kind of a permanent oratorical quantity, a thing in itself, compared by Thompson to General Douglas MacArthur's "Old Soldiers Never Die" address to Congress in 1951.

As you wander, abashed and amazed, through the four pages of this document, you cannot help saying to yourself that it is a speech by which Jimmy Carter can be tested

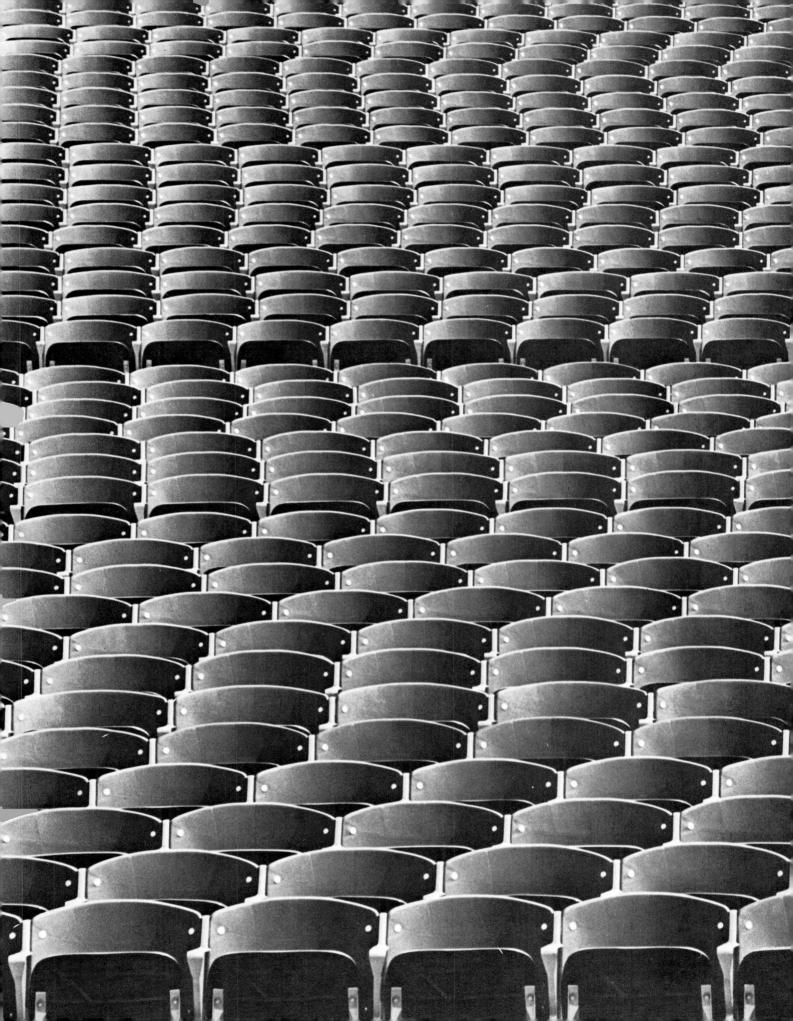

eight or ten years from now, which would be ten or twelve years after he gave it. In other words, it is a speech that could last at least a decade, if only to put Jimmy himself to the proof.

He is talking to lawyers, Jimmy is, and he is talking in the midst of the Watergate revelations, and he is talking also about the rights of human beings.

"My own interest in the criminal justice system is very deep and heartfelt. Not having studied law, I've had to learn the hard way. I read a lot and listen a lot . . .

"Well, as a farmer who has now been in office for three years, I've seen first-hand the inadequacy of my own comprehension of what government ought to do for its people. I've had a constant learning process, sometimes from lawyers, sometimes from practical experience, sometimes from failures and mistakes that have been pointed out to me after they were made.

"I had lunch this week with the members of the Judicial Selection Committee, and they were talking about a consent search warrant. I said I didn't know what a consent search warrant was. They said, 'Well, that's when two policemen go to a house. One of them goes to the front door and knocks on it, and the other one runs around to the back door and yells "come in." ' "

As Governor, Jimmy goes on to admit, he had often played the same game—not pushing the law as hard as all

that but trying to make the law work the way he wanted it to. He talks about what he is trying to do to improve the criminal justice system in the State of Georgia, saying that when he, a legal layman, analyzed some of the sentences given to people by the Superior Court judges, they grieved him deeply and shocked him. He talks about making distinctions among various kinds of crimes relating to drugs and alcohol, then says: "We've finally been able to get through the legislature a law that removes alcoholism or drunkenness as a criminal offense. When this law goes into effect next year, I think it will create a new sense of compassion and concern and justice for the roughly 150,000 alcoholics in Georgia." He talks about efforts to straighten out the prison system and the GBI (Georgia Bureau of Investigation). "Well," Jimmy asks after noting these accomplishments, "does that mean that everything is all right?" then says:

"It doesn't to me.

"I don't know exactly how to say this, but I was thinking just a few moments ago about some of the things that are of deep concern to me as Governor. As a scientist, I was working constantly, along with almost everyone who professes that dedication of life, to probe, probe every day of my life for constant change for the better. It's completely anachronistic in [he means antipathetic to] the makeup of a nuclear physicist or an engineer or scientist to be satisfied with what we've got, or to rest on the laurels of past accomplishments. It's the nature of the profession . . .

"Every farmer that I know of," he goes on to say, "who is worth his salt or who's just average, is ahead of the experiment stations and the research agronomist in finding

better ways, changing ways to plant, cultivate, utilize herbicides, gather, cure, sell farm products. The competition for innovation is tremendous, equivalent to the realm of nuclear physics even."

Maybe, though, it's different, he says—in a kind of murderously innocent swipe at lawyers. Maybe the legal profession isn't supposed to find ever better ways to do its job. Then, with the same kind of lethal innocence in his tone, Jimmy Carter reviews the religious underpinnings of law: "I'm a Sunday school teacher, and I've always known that the structure of law is founded on the Christian ethic that you shall love the Lord your God and your neighbor as yourself—a very high and perfect standard. We all know [that] the fallibility of man, and the contentions in society, as described by Reinhold Niebuhr and many others, don't

permit us to achieve perfection." And he launches into a polite attack on "the powerful and the influential" and the unwillingness of these people to rock the boat of the status quo.

Next he produces a homely example to illustrate what he is suggesting about the stupidity of refusing to accept useful change.

"I remember when I was a child, I lived on a farm about three miles from Plains, and we didn't have electricity or running water. We lived on the railroad—Seaboard Coastline railroad. Like all farm boys I had a flip, a sling shot. They had stabilized the railroad bed with little white round rocks, which I used for ammunition. I would go out frequently to the railroad and gather the most perfectly shaped rocks of proper size. I always had a few in my pockets, and I had others cached away around the farm, so that they would be convenient if I ran out of my pocket supply.

"One day I was leaving the railroad track with my pockets full of rocks and hands full of rocks, and my mother came out on the front porch—this is not a very interesting story but it illustrates a point—and she had in her hands a plate full of cookies that she had just baked for me. She called me, I am sure with love in her heart, and said, 'Jimmy, I've baked some cookies for you.' I remember very distinctly walking up to her and standing there for fifteen or twenty seconds, in honest doubt about whether I should

drop those rocks which were worthless and take the cookies that my mother had prepared for me, which between her and me were very valuable."

"We don't recognize that change can sometimes be very beneficial," he says, and talks about the embarrassment of "the last fifteen or twenty years" in the South, and what a horrible thing it would be to try "to forego the one man, one vote principle"—to go backwards—in "horrible violation of the basic principles of justice and equality and fairness and equity."

He next talks about the speech he made in the State Senate to help get the "thirty questions" abolished, and then about "Martin Luther King, Jr., who was perhaps despised by many in this room because he shook up our social structure . . . and demanded simply that black citizens be treated the same as white citizens . . . He was greeted with horror. Still, once that change was made, a very simple but difficult change, no one in his right mind would want to go back to circumstances prior . . ."

Then once again Jimmy Carter reemphasizes his main point. He realizes, he says, that he is part of the system or the problem.

"But, the point I want to make to you is that we still have a long way to go. In every age or every year, we have a tendency to believe that we've come so far now, that there's

no way to improve the present system. I'm sure when the Wright Brothers flew at Kitty Hawk, they felt that was the ultimate in transportation . . .

"Well, we haven't reached the ultimate. But who's going to search the heart and the soul of an organization like yours or a law school or state or nation and say, 'What can we still do to restore equity and justice or to preserve it or to enhance it in this society?'

"You know, I'm not afraid to make the change. I don't have anything to lose. But, as a farmer I'm not qualified to assess the characteristics of the ninety-one hundred inmates in the Georgia prisons, 50 percent of whom ought not to be there. They ought to be on probation or under some other supervision and assess what the results of previous court rulings might bring to bear on their lives.

"I was in the Governor's Mansion for two years, enjoying the services of a very fine cook, who was a prisoner—a woman. One day she came to me, after she got over her two years of timidity, and said, 'Governor, I would like to borrow $250 from you.'

"I said, 'I'm not sure that a lawyer would be worth that much.'

"She said, 'I don't want to hire a lawyer, I want to pay the judge.'

"I thought it was a ridiculous statement for her; I felt that she was ignorant. But I found out she wasn't. She had been sentenced by a Superior Court judge in the state, who still serves, to seven years or $750. She had raised, early in her prison career, $500. I didn't lend her the money, but I had Bill Harper, my legal aide, look into it. He found the circumstances were true. She was quickly released under a recent court ruling that had come down in the last few years.

"I was down on the coast this weekend. I was approached by a woman who asked me to come by her home. I went by, and she showed me documents that indicated that her illiterate mother, who had a son in jail, had gone to the

104

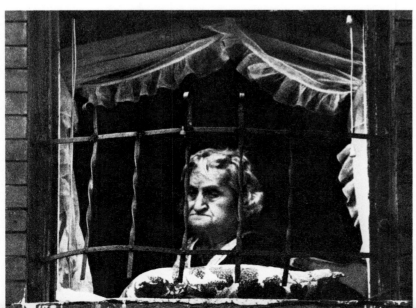

County Surveyor in that region and had borrowed $225 to get her son out of jail. She had a letter from the Justice of the Peace that showed that her mother had made a mark on a blank sheet of paper. They paid off the $225, and she has the receipts to show it. Then they started a five-year program trying to get back the paper she signed, without success. They went to court. The lawyer that had originally advised her to sign the paper showed up as the attorney for the Surveyor. She had put up fifty acres of land near the county seat as security. When she got to court she found that instead of signing a security deed, that she had signed a warranty deed. That case has already been appealed to the Supreme Court, and she lost."

And Jimmy Carter goes on to say, "You can go in the prisons of Georgia, and—I don't know, it may be that poor people are the only ones who commit crimes, but I do know they are the only ones who serve prison sentences. When Ellis MacDougall first went to Reidsville, he found people that had been in solitary confinement for ten years . . ."

Then Jimmy says: "Well, I don't know the theory of law, but there is one other point I want to make, just for

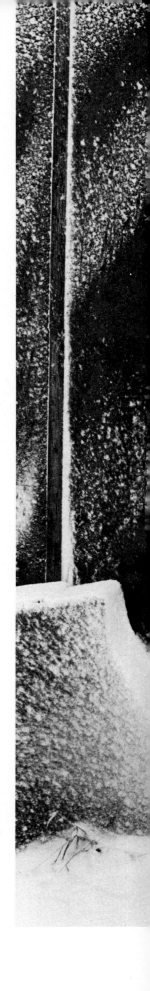

your own consideration . . . Just think for a moment about your own son or your own father or your own daughter being in prison, having served seven years of a lifetime term and being considered for a release. Don't you think that they ought to be examined and that the Pardons and Paroles Board ought to look them in the eye and ask them a question and, if they are turned down, ought to give them some substantive reason why they are not released and what they can do to correct their defect?

"I do.

"I think it's just as important . . . as it is . . . when they are sentenced. But, I don't know how to bring about that change."

He talks about how, when he and the Georgia legislature were trying to get an ethics bill passed, it was the lawyers who were the largest force against it. Then:

"The regulatory agencies in Washington are made up, not of people to regulate industries, but of representatives of the industries that are regulated. Is that fair and right and equitable? I don't think so.

"I'm only going to serve four years as Governor, as you know. I think that's enough. I enjoy it, but I think I've done

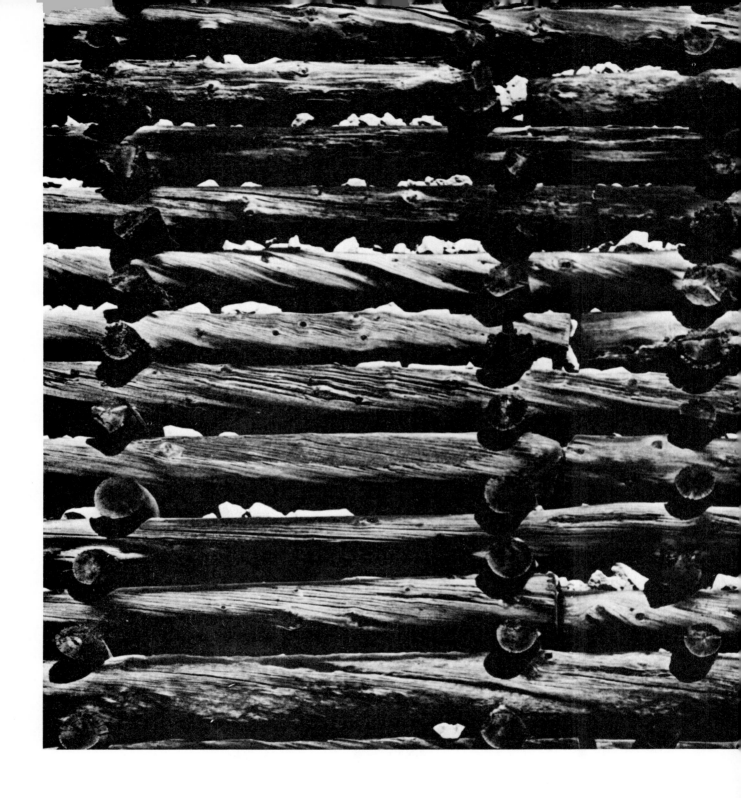

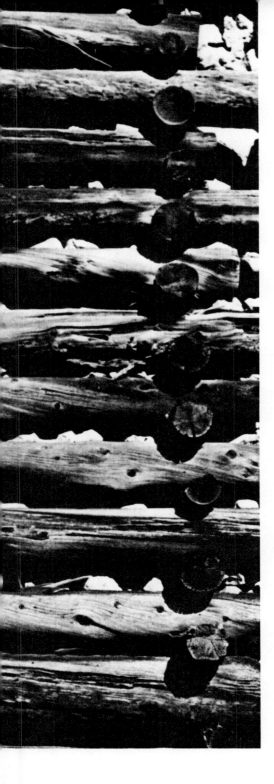

all I can in the Governor's office. I see the lobbyists in the State Capitol filling the halls on occasions. Good people, competent people, the most pleasant, personable, extroverted citizens of Georgia. Those are the characteristics that are required for a lobbyist. They represent good folks. But I tell you that when a lobbyist goes to represent the Peanut Warehousemen's Association of the Southeast, which I belong to, which I helped to organize, they go there to represent the peanut warehouseman. They don't go there to represent the customers of the peanut warehouseman.

"When the State Chamber of Commerce lobbyists go there, they go there to represent the businessman of Georgia. They don't go there to represent the customers of the businessman of Georgia . . .

"The American Medical Association and its Georgia equivalent—they represent the doctors, who are fine people. But they certainly don't represent the patients of a doctor.

"As an elected Governor, I feel that responsibility; but I also know that my qualifications are slight compared to the

doctors or the lawyers or the teachers, to determine what's best for the client or the patient or the school child.

"This bothers me; and I know that if there was a commitment on the part of the cumulative group of attorneys in this State, to search with a degree of commitment and fervency, to eliminate many of the inequities that I've just described that I thought of this morning, our state could be transformed in the attitude of its people toward the government.

"Senator Kennedy described the malaise that exists in this nation, and it does . . ."

Then Jimmy tells a story—and you suddenly wish he would tell more such stories. This story shows, as much as anything Jimmy Carter has ever said, the roots of his sincerity and his compassion, when they are real and active

and alive in his mind. There are times now when you wonder whether, instead of giving a particular speech, or repeating the same material, Jimmy would rather be back home in Plains, sitting in silence and thinking about the problems and getting back in touch with that reservoir of human awareness from which fresh compassionate insights can emerge.

"When I was about twelve years old, I liked to read, and I had a school principal, named Miss Julia Coleman. Judge Marshall knows her. She forced me pretty much to read, read, read, classical books. She would give me a gold star when I read ten and a silver star when I read five.

"One day, she called me in and she said, 'Jimmy, I think it's time for you to read WAR AND PEACE.' I was completely relieved because I thought it was a book about cowboys and Indians.

"Well, I went to the library and checked it out, and it was 1,415 pages thick, I think—written by Tolstoy, as you know, about Napoleon's entry into Russia in the 1812–1815 era. He had never been defeated and he was sure he could win, but he underestimated the severity of the Russian winter and the peasants' love for their land.

"To make a long story short, the next spring he retreated in defeat. The course of history was changed; it probably affected our own lives.

"The point of the book is, and what Tolstoy points out in the epilogue is, that he didn't write the book about Napoleon or the Czar of Russia or even the generals, except in a rare occasion. He wrote it about the students and the housewives and the barbers and the farmers and the privates in the Army. And the point of the book is that the course of human events, even the greatest historical events, are not determined by the leaders of a nation or a state, like presidents or governors or senators. They are controlled by the combined wisdom and courage and commitment and discernment and unselfishness and compassion and love and idealism of the common ordinary people. If that was true in the case of Russia where they had a czar or France where they had an emperor, how much more true

is it in our own case where the Constitution charges us with a direct responsibility for determining what our government is and ought to be?"

Then the image comes to your mind of the deposed Richard Nixon, who wanted to appear pious, who wanted to surprise them all and be a great president, but who—not entirely unlike his sponsor Dwight D. Eisenhower—was so caught up with his image and his own self. And then you think of the disdain for the unfortunates of society, or certainly at least disinterest in their problems and concerns. This from the party of Abraham Lincoln? You think

of Barbara Jordan, at the 1976 Convention, saying Democrats' mistakes were mistakes of the heart. Well, real Democrats eh? And how real Democrats are emotionally driven, as far as human sense can be driven, toward concern for human beings: This is the Democratic trumpet call and battle cry that echoes in the mind. And you see

that Jimmy Carter is sincere, and you think maybe he can never be anything but sincere, if on a day like that, with apparently nothing to gain, he could turn almost platitudinous language into a proud restatement of the American creed:

"Well, I've read parts of the embarrassing transcripts, and I've seen the proud statement of a former attorney general, who protected his boss, and now brags on the fact that he tiptoed through a mine field and came out 'clean.' I can't imagine somebody like Thomas Jefferson tiptoeing through a mine field on the technicalities of the law, and then bragging about being clean afterwards.

"I think our people demand more than that. I believe that everyone in this room who is in a position of responsibility as a preserver of the law in its purest form ought to remember the oath that Thomas Jefferson and others took when they practically signed their own death warrant, writing the Declaration of Independence—to preserve justice and equity and freedom and fairness, they pledged their lives, their fortunes and their sacred honor.

"Thank you very much."

And so you're pretty well finished shuffling through those musty files, and you want to say that the whole Jimmy Carter search exercise so far seems to have been worthwhile. What next emerges is strange enough—the sharpened awareness that Jimmy Carter is a man so rooted and grounded in compassion that he can make political capital of this compassion. Sure, he knows it will work for him, and get him votes. But he has a right, doesn't he, to those votes? Because he knows this compassionate sense is a permanent extra eye inside him—a fixed resource, like a deep well or a Providence Spring or like one of those biblical unquenchable fires. He knows that he can honestly and sincerely talk about his own compassion, even when he can—with honesty and sincerity and conviction—talk about nothing else. He may have his problems—explaining, for example, how he is going to satisfy both conservative economists and social liberals—how he can save money and yet spend money. He will say he has an "econometric model" set up in some computer, busily churning out figures and estimates. Perhaps it's real. Maybe he thinks he can spend more money, yet in the end save still more money and balance the budget, by simply eliminating waste. Whether he can do this must, at least at times, be open to question even in his own head.

But why should Jimmy Carter ever doubt the reality of his sense of compassion? He can make political capital of this until the crack of doom, or at least until he comes home to the cows: because—you can tell from the ring of that Law Day speech, you hope—he knows in his heart, that he has that deep vein of compassion, as much a part of him as the throbbing vein in his temple his mother Lillian likes to talk about. The man has a genuine feeling about people who are poor, oppressed, and downtrodden. But, if this is true, and if this compassion is also the number one gut reality about Jimmy Carter, then an awful lot follows.

Whether or not Jimmy Carter was one of the best governors in Georgia history, as his friends claim, what did happen was that during his years in the mansion at Atlanta, as a leading political personality in the South, Jimmy was visited rather regularly in 1971 and afterward by people who were active or prospective candidates for President. He watched them come and go. He watched some of them booze it up. He assessed their quality, and it began to occur to him, and to his wife Rosalynn and to his close advisers, that perhaps he was better suited for the awesome office of the Presidency than they. Jimmy Carter was temperate, he worked hard; he was intelligent, he had certain inner resources. It was possible that the Era of Reconstruction, and of two-way carpetbagging, was finally over, and that an attractive candidate from the South could actually have a shot at the Presidency. For two years they talked about it, Rosalynn says. Once Jimmy had made up his mind, the Carter machine wiped its sweaty brow, rolled up its sleeves, and swung into action, guided by the political cunning of the principal and the country con of his advisers—men like Hamilton Jordan, Jody Powell, and the courtly Charles Kirbo.

Jimmy Carter seems not to be ruthless, if ruthlessness be defined as kicking in the teeth of anyone who stands on

the ladder with you. But he is a determined man. Once the Carter mind is made up, there is that relentlessness. (Later Jimmy would talk of Kissinger's Lone Ranger diplomacy—a little unfairly, because the William Tell Overture could have been written for Jimmy himself.) Once the target is in place, all capabilities are brought into play.

Jimmy sought and was awarded, by Democratic Party Chairman Robert Strauss, the national chairmanship of the off-year Democratic congressional campaign in 1974. So Jimmy Carter traveled the country, helping candidates and

making friends. Then late that year, the word went forth from Plains, Atlanta, and Washington that upon leaving the governorship Jimmy Carter was going to run for the Presidency of the United States.

He was the earliest candidate to categorically announce his absolute intention of going for broke, and by the

Spring of 1975 he was out across the country, talking about his vision of America, and soliciting people's views. It was alleged that he was a man who took polls before taking positions. But he did seem, even then, to be a man who knew where his head was. This country was okay after all; even George McGovern had given America, and Jimmy, something—a more open Democratic primary process.

Long before—in 1972, when he was considering this crazy project of running for the Presidency itself—Jimmy had begun to gather foreign policy advisors and to shape an approach to international questions.

By late 1975, after a long trudge across the Nixieford wasteland, Jimmy Carter had come from nowhere to be considered among the top half dozen or so leading Democratic candidates in the nation. It was widely assumed that he would be killed off somehow along the way. But he won an early caucus in Iowa in January 1976, and the advertisements of this victory—especially by R. W. Apple of the NEW YORK TIMES—gave him an impetus he had no intention of losing. The caucus in Mississippi voted strongly for Wallace against Jimmy. It was difficult and sometimes depressing going, but in New Hampshire on February 24, Jimmy Carter got more than thirty percent of the vote against a field of candidates, and won in a Northern state—a small state, but it was the first primary, and a primary Mo Udall or one of the other hopefuls might easily have won.

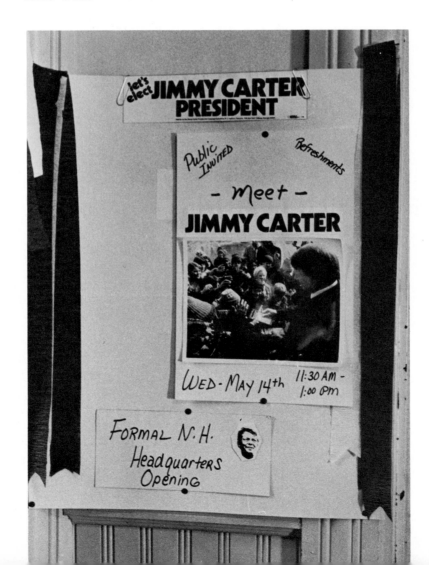

There were successes and defeats after that, but with New Hampshire suddenly it was Jimmy Carter—and not Scoop Jackson or any of the other candidates—whom people thought maybe, and Hubert Humphrey thought maybe, Hubert would have to make a deal with before he settled into the candidacy at the Democratic Convention in July.

Jimmy lost in Massachusetts while winning in Florida against George Wallace. Scotty Reston of the TIMES was

now talking up a vice-presidency for Carter, in the hope against hope that this Southerner would not (oh, never a South Georgian!) be President himself. He won in Illinois (against Wallace), then lost in New York, then won again in North Carolina (against Wallace), and suddenly it was time for the crunch: Pennsylvania.

Here the larger number of Democratic city machines and bosses and virtually all the labor leaders got behind Scoop Jackson—some or most of them to lay the way for Jackson's departure and Humphrey's coronation. But Jimmy Carter and his peanut brigade of "Georgians for

Jimmy" got their message to the people in that huge and Northern state, and when election night returns were in in Pennsylvania, Jimmy had trounced Scoop Jackson. It was a very big victory.

Suddenly people were saying that Jimmy was not only the man to beat, but was now almost unstoppable. Congressman Andrew Young thought so. Young was the leader who, after Daddy King—Martin Luther King, Sr.—had given Jimmy the black support of greatest value. Andy Young said something to the effect that the only thing that could stop Jimmy now was to attack a nun, on the steps of the Capitol, at high noon—"and then lie about it."

But the Northern and Western liberal barbarians came charging in against the Carter candidacy. Good grief, a Southerner! A serious Christian! Insolent and insidious! A new sort of reverse racism combined now with the spluttering self-interest of sundry vested egos, in a Holy War against Carter. Suddenly, in Jerry Brown, they had a candidate ("See Jimmy run! I can run!") who could make anti-establishment noises but who seemed suddenly so much more cozily familiar than this South Georgian—this Jimmy Carter. Frank Church emerged from his calm deliberations about the depradations of CIA and FBI, to throw his hat happily into the ring. Brown swept to a beauty contest—popular vote—victory in Maryland. Church recorded some signal, if modest, successes in the West. Screaming headlines: CARTER STUMBLES! But, alas! As pore Jimmy Carter stumbled, week by week he added delegates by the ten dozen.

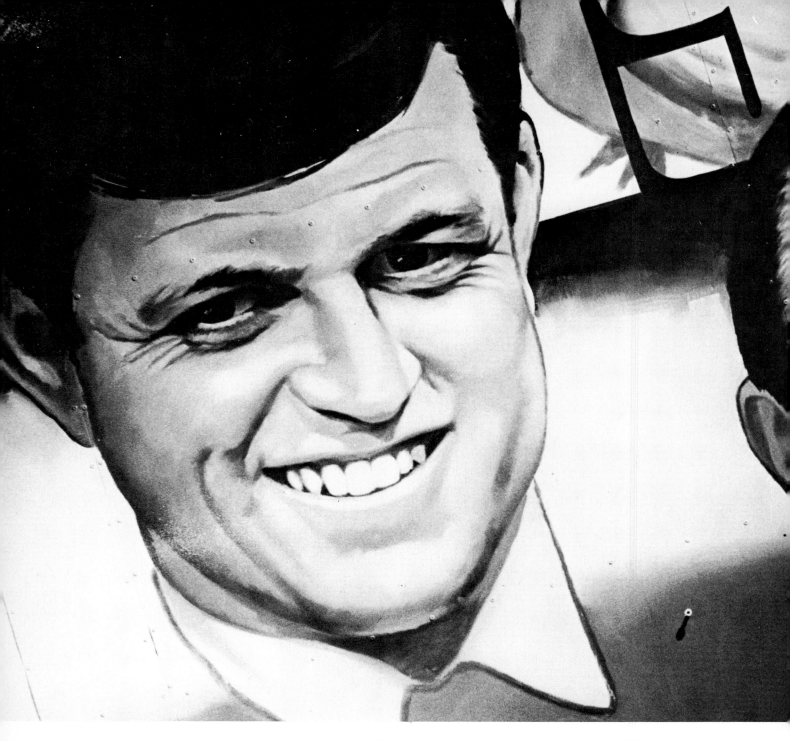

Jimmy's delegate total was mounting like mercury at the equator. The anti-Carter forces began to make violent last ditch organizational noises, with a tearful but available Hubert Humphrey as their probable ultimate candidate. Suddenly one Saturday, in May, the hint of a new kind of dream ticket—Humphrey-Kennedy! Fantastic! (Was Carter that dangerous?) Teddy, when asked about Jimmy Carter, said, "I hardly know the man." Teddy was at a loss like everybody else to explain—and he could not approve— the Carter surge. Authoritatively, that Saturday in May, the NEW YORK DAILY NEWS said Teddy would accept a draft. The ball game! Carter finished? But wait! What does Teddy

himself say? Would he consider running after all? Of course
Ted Kennedy denied it. Kennedy had no intention of running, either at the top of the ticket, or the bottom. Death
was not on his bicentennial agenda.

Great-hearted man, but had Teddy missed out on what
was happening? He wanted to stop Jimmy, it now appeared, or at least to force Jimmy to consider the message
the liberals were trying to send him: Jimmy, Jimmy, listen
to the people! Now, here is how reality must be thought
about by a Democrat in modern America. But Jimmy, who
genuinely loved the poor and downtrodden, apparently was

the newer and more modern Democrat, or the Democrat whose ear was better tuned to the problems of the post-Nixon era—more keenly aware of the time's demands than Hubert Horatio Humphrey—the Happy Warrior of days gone by—or than Ted Kennedy himself.

> They said, You have a blue guitar,
> You do not play things as they are.
> The man replied, Things as they are
> Are changed upon the blue guitar.

So Jimmy Carter went surging on, and it gradually dawned on all concerned that Jimmy Carter's weight of delegates was beginning to scale in very heavily; so heavily that the ABC (anybody but Carter) movement was now looking more and more like a frenzied, frantic, leaderless last lurch. But wait! They would roll Jerry Brown and Hubert Humphrey up into a Jersey beach ball, and smack Jimmy with it. The test would come on Super Tuesday when New Jersey, Ohio, and California—good old suburban superpopular zen Catholic Jerry Brown's California—would all trot off to the polls. Aha! Jimmy was supposed to win in New Jersey. But a coalition of uncommitted delegates, backing both Humphrey and Brown, would beat him there.

They did! Victory? Carter at last destroyed? In California, it was Jerry Brown's best day since Maryland. He rolled up more than two hundred California delegates! But, pouf! The California victory, on behalf of favorite son Brown, was expected. And in Jersey, well—whoever uncommitted delegates think they are really pledged to (Humphrey? Brown? Unknown Somewho?), they are, after all, delegates listed as uncommitted. In Ohio (O pity and indignation!) it was Jimmy Carter all the way, knocking both Church and Udall (grumble) out of the box. Jerry Brown's late-racing strategy ("A little vagueness goes a long way") became as so much flapping in the wind. Brown's very approach had been meant to suggest Jimmy Carter's capital O Opportunism. But Jimmy had played his opportunities like a chess master, had moved very carefully and worked very hard across the whole board. Besides, on the way to losing those uncommitted delegates, Jimmy Carter had won the popularity contest in New Jersey. White flags went up, from the redwood forests (of the Northwest, anyway) to the New York island.

It was all over now, except for the march to Jimmy's flag. Officially first in to salute the Peanut King of the Universe, was Mayor Dick Daley of Chicago, who had for weeks been making friendly mumbles about Carter ("By God, you've got to admire him"). Then Governor George Wallace of Alabama (Wow!), then Senators Humphrey and Church and Jackson, and then, eventually, all the others—in a slowly building snowball in June and July. Strangely enough, the liberals—who should have seen the

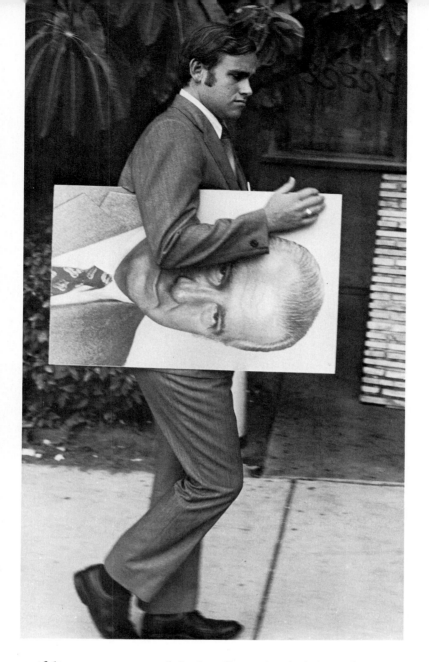

gutfelt compassion and the hardly concealed thirst for progress in Jimmy Carter's whole person and strategy—were
the last to drag in. And the Kennedys, who had survived the
same kind of fight a decade and a half earlier—why were
they so slow to accept him?

A new kind of phenomenon had occurred in American
Democratic politics. Here was a personal conservative of
profoundly liberal spirit; a man of tremendous energy who
by careful planning and hard work had risen to earned
leadership: a man who might actually unify the national
party, and who would begin to stir the nation with a feeling
that he was the man needed to undo all the damage done by
Wayne Hays and Watergate, the leader to drive the
Nixiepublicans at last out of office: the man who might even
move the country once and for all beyond all that—out into
the future, where the blight of the Nixon-Agnew era would
recede into dim memory . . .

Part 3
Who is Jimmy Carter?

In which the visitor attempts to explore some of the bizarre questions that have been raised or willy-nilly must be raised, concerning the most extraordinary candidacy that has occurred in a very long while: questions spiritual and political, emotional and psychiatric—innocent, insolent and weird questions, about experience and innocence, sincerity and deception, cunning and compassion, about intelligence and unremitting toil, about love and anger and personal morality, relentless ambition and religious faith.

As the visitor to Georgia, on a respite from his prowls around Plains, sits in his air-conditioned motel room in Americus, and tries to figure out the Carter proposition as a whole, he has to be aware of the goings and comings from time to time of members of the national press—or "the media" as this group is collectively called in the clumsy idiom of the age. Rarely do any of the truly famous drop in down here. But of those who do appear—as with the famous—some are people of broader rather than limited view. Anyway, among them are some very good folks.

A press group can be—depending on the mix of people and the mood and the hour and the news—a hotbox of analysis. Sometimes the very nothingness of the news hottens the box. But the people of the press are there to find out what's going on—even if the strictures of reporting won't let them tell. Many newsfolk are cynical. Some few are hostile, or assume a pose of hostility. Many (most?) are friendly, and wish Jimmy Carter well. But even some who are enthusiasts for Jimmy Carter above all other presidential candidates worry about his personality.

Among these journalists are those who have been close to Jimmy Carter before—in Atlanta or on the campaign trail—and yet feel uneasy about him. They find something unfathomable in Jimmy Carter, and it troubles them. Now a cautious if partisan observer may expostulate with the hostiles, or even with the critical friendlies. But the problem—or problems—will not go away.

What bothers some members of the press is a temperamentalism that ill accords, they feel, with Jimmy's public profession of affection and love for all mankind. They are annoyed by his occasional snappishness or his reluctance to make the right gestures. But there is talk too of a magnanimity in him. This comes out in different ways, and sometimes when least expected. The trip to Montgomery to thank George Wallace for his endorsement some thought an extraordinarily gracious gesture. No doubt there is room here for greater effort. Perhaps the moments of annoyance have something to do with rest and sleep and the lack of these. Once Carter has launched into the work that he has set himself to do—the work of improving the country's

government—those close to him will no doubt see that he gets more rest so that his moments in the sun are sunny moments, not shadowed by pique.

The problem of getting at Jimmy is further complicated by this desperate effort—as it appears—to make him presentable. There is for one example the managed (modular, TV) haircut. One suspects that Jimmy is not at all vain about his appearance. But it is as though Jimmy's handlers are in odd moments frightened to death that his plainness might occur to a public yearning for the edged features of Camelot. Or, in another mood of fear, they seem to worry that people would forget about his plainness, and think of him as the very smooth political practitioner he actually is.

There is also, and up on Track A, The Case of the Unnatural Smile. The intrusive television cameras in his hotel room the night of his nomination brought the nation horribly face to face in profile with the wrong smile. Still photographs cannot convey the grisliness of the experience. It was especially and terribly embarrassing during the long minutes when Rosalynn was pouring her heart out, in a soul-shatteringly moving way, to the greedy outthrust television microphones and cameras. And Jimmy was required by the rules of this peeping tom fool voyeuristic TV game to sit there smiling at her—and at his TV image smiling at her!—as she vividly and heartbreakingly talked of what she and Jimmy had been through together. These people should have some privacy, even when their determined commitment to what they are doing makes them forget that they need privacy.

152

154

But then the night of his acceptance speech, the following night, Jimmy smiled appropriately—smiled, it appeared, when he felt like smiling, when he was actually naturally normally moved to smile. Of course that night, most of the time, as a serious man saying serious things, he was sober, solemn—sometimes even understandably angry. He entered fully and honestly into that performance as a performance. Jimmy Carter has a good smile—a variety of good smiles. When you meet him he blazes with convincing friendliness. By all accounts he actually and truly likes to smile. But one cannot—especially if one is as serious about his business as this fellow is—smile benignly the whole while. There should be no more required smiles! Amy, his daughter, knows this. No more forced smiles! It is as painful for the smilee as it must be for the smiler.

So, you think: Maybe it is time for all concerned to quit playing with images and give us Jimmy Carter himself. This hokum hick business and the unreal smiles are part of what confuses smarter people. The real Jimmy Carter is straight and civil when not downright charming. But he's no chucklehead. Surely in his new line of work, now that he has arrived or is about to, there will be less felt need to smile so much. In this new job, like his close friend the Holy Spirit,

He comes with work to do, he does not come to coo,
He comes to brood and sit.

Jimmy, in and of himself, is readily enough perceived as wholesome. For instance, there are these thoughts from a down-home witness:

"Here is what is so appalling, here is what so stumped the experts. Never has one man so quietly and so tactfully and diplomatically organized a campaign as Jimmy and his workers did. So, out of the South, the eleven states that have been the whipping dogs of the United States of America, comes a man of high caliber, a gentleman, the progeny of good breeding, who can go and talk with kings and not lose the common touch. He's an educated man, he's an experienced man. He gave us a good honest record in Georgia.

"Jimmy was nurtured on the knee of a happy mother, a happy father. He was wanted when he was born, he was loved. He was taught to grow up and respect everyone. For a person that has not caught the blessing, the feeling, of realizing that if I accept Christ as my Savior, I can accept that man across town today who's black and hungry, that white man across town who's a pauper whom society will have nothing to do with—that may be hard to understand . . .

"There are Southerners who have money, who have inherited estates, who don't want anybody but 'me and mine' to have it. 'Just don't let that other family get their foot in the door! I know them blacks—let's just keep them up in back!' But thank God that Jimmy Carter speaks the language that people are hungry for, people who have accepted Christ as their personal Savior. It's love. It's grace. It's 'I am my brother's keeper.' Jimmy says—and I know he feels it: 'When I was in prison, you visited me; when I was hungry you fed me; when I was sick you came to see me.' And he went across town like the Good Samaritan. He went into the bushes and the byways where they were lying there hungry, where they were in need. That boy on that back porch is my blood brother, but he's not any more my brother than that black man down there in colored town. 'I am your keeper, if you need me today.' And I feel in my heart that that's what Jimmy Carter's got on his mind."

A wanderer through the Western reaches of South

Georgia can hardly pass through Lumpkin, or reconstructed Westville—"where it's always 1850"—without meeting Miss Pattie Price Pearson. She's a local personality—a lady whose people have lived down there a long time. Her home is at 1 Main Street in Lumpkin. She's a pianist who plays "Amazin' Grace" like an angel, and she can tell you a story or make you a preachment that will make your peanuts boil and your grits stand on end. She's also a Jimmy Carter sympathizer, and evangelical about it.

"In one of his first appearances Jimmy said, 'I will never tell you a lie.' This goes back to something that is inherent in his being, in his roots. It's just natural, it's just there. Jimmy is a man who is known for his honesty. There was nothing shady about his government when he was Governor. And as a Senator he was known by those with

whom he worked to be a man of trust, a man of honor, and a man of honest government.

"Jimmy is a man that can supply the needs of people verbally, orally, over the networks. When he gets to Washington, he's a man who's going to speak for everybody. He is not beholden to the rich or the status Joneses, or those on the inside track in Washington, D.C. He did it the hard way . . .

"Jimmy has always had a feeling, as I see it, for his fellowman, and he's going to get votes out there in America. He's going straight into that White House, because people are sick of Watergate, cow gate, horse gate. You name the gate, they're sick of it . . .

"Over in Plains, Georgia, we've got a leader. If it's God's

will, he's going to lead us. Now, he can't please everybody all the time. But I think he can do the absolute most for the nation at present . . .

"When he gets in that White House, Jimmy's not going to moralize. No sir, he won't have time for that. He'll go right on. He's not going to try to push his religion down your throat. He's going to let his light shine. He will set an example. And he will go up there—and he has the brains, he has the stamina, to hold his own with them. He's a high-type man. The country's ready for a change. And, in my book, Jimmy's the man of the hour. Now is the time for people to be serious, and to get together, pull together. Let's have harmony in the nation. Down here we call it grits, a lot of people call it hominy . . .

"Jimmy's not going to get trigger-happy but he's going to be very tough. He's a man of tough fiber. He's a man that's hard-headed. He's not going to cater to this one or that one. What does he owe those men sitting up there? He owes them nothing but a 'Good day, sir. How are you today? Hi, you-all, here in the U.S. Senate. Hi, you-all, there in the House of Representatives.' He's going into that Oval Office, into his chambers. He's going to go with perception, acumen. He's a man just filled with history, statistics, things that have happened not only in Plains, Georgia, and South Georgia, and Atlanta, but North, East, South, West—he's a well-read man. We want to thank him for what he's done for the South. He has helped to sound our trumpet out in the country, and show them that a man can dress up in a handsome outfit with wing-tipped shoes and a beautiful tie and shirt, and a clean head, and a clean body, and a clean mind. You don't give me many men with a clean mind and a clean body. He loves Rosalynn. He's been true to Rosalynn. He brought those children into the world, and he set an example. He's kept God's commandment. He took that wedding vow. He's kept it. He's had his mind on his Lord's business, he's had his mind on his family, on making a living, helping the State of Georgia, and now he wants to heal the wounds of America, and come out with a wonderful package of happiness.

"Is he going to admonish us all to follow Christ? No, but he would set the example of following Christ . . . There will be that witness. But he's going to be known by his fruits. He has had a fruitful life from the time he was a little boy attending church. Witnessing, teaching.

"He's the man of the hour. I believe that fate has deemed him the man in the right place at the right time, and I think when he is elected President, after he is nominated as the Democratic nominee he will take up the reins of government and he will put it all back together and we will have harmony and peace."

That is Pattie Price Pearson's answer to the question who Jimmy Carter is. Few of the home folk are as eloquent

as she. But there's her friend Maxine Reese, who has been running Jimmy's depot office in Plains since it opened on Easter Sunday, 1976. She is in fact the founding mother. Maxine perceives Jimmy partly through her own work for him, helping him. She's getting a special train organized to take the local people right on up to Washington for the inaugural day ceremonies. Maxine says of Jimmy:

"He was a good Governor for the State of Georgia, and I've known him twenty years, and given the fact that he is a Southerner from my hometown—of course, I wanted to work for him. You've got to believe in him. I thought he was qualified to do the job, and I knew he needed some help, and I had some time and was willing to do it.

"He didn't pick me out of all these people. I picked him. I was the one that wanted to do it. I talked to the people downtown who ran the businesses, I talked to Rosalynn, and Rosalynn in turn would talk to Jimmy. She said the warehouse business had a lease on the depot, and that she knew we needed an office in Plains. The people sort of looked to me and expected me to do it. So I went to Billy and said that we should have an office in Plains, where people could go and get information and directions and buttons and things. So Billy and I got busy and cleaned up the depot. We got the front office fixed first. Billy saw that I was really determined. John Pope came in with his steam cleaner and

cleaned all the freight room and part of the outside. And Martha Jean Glasscock and Betty Pope came in. One thing led to another and volunteers came in. Even before the grand opening on Easter Sunday, people were coming in. I told Rosalynn that it was ready and that we wanted Jimmy to speak, and he came down and opened it. After that we had primary parties on Tuesday nights. The local ladies would bake things and we'd have nonalcoholic punch. It got to be just a community activity . . .

"Jimmy wasn't always there—sometimes he'd just call in. But Miz Lillian would come, and Billy and Hugh and all the Carter people. It was exciting. The only primary party Jimmy attended was the last one, when he won big in Ohio. That was a special night. There was a statewide celebration—a victory party. We sold tickets, but you could get in without one. We had a band, refreshments, we had a street dance planned, two singing groups. He didn't get there till about 1:30 a.m. and when he got there and got out of the car, that whole crowd—the street was full of people—was singing 'God Bless America.' Some people said it was the most moving experience they'd ever had in their lives. Some said they had tears in their eyes. Jimmy was laughing, his smile was just ear-to-ear. John Pope— who had been his friend for years—Jimmy ran up and bear-hugged him. Jimmy and Rosalynn were just tickled to death, glad to be home, exhausted . . ."

Maxine Reese is a large, buxom, incredibly warm woman; a depot-shaking laugh issues from her every two or three minutes. She is one of those salt-of-the-earth people—a little like the younger Kate Smith. She is a native of Early County, Georgia, but her personality is an all-embracing one—as large as the country she wants to see Jimmy Carter lead.

"Jimmy has an inner feeling of security and dedication. He has peace with himself. He draws inner strength from this . . . It's something most people don't understand, that they shouldn't have any fear, ever . . . Jimmy's going to bring concern. He wants us to have concern for one another, to treat one another as brothers, and love one another—meaning that we work things out together in a calm atmosphere . . . Everything will be out in the open with him, working for the good of the country and of the country's people, bettering the standard of living for everybody. He speaks of love. I think love is concern, compassion. Respect has a lot to do with it . . . We're all different in some respects, but basically people are alike. They want the same things—a good living, a comfortable home, nice kids, a happy family. And they want love. A man or woman that's got love, they can do anything . . ."

One wishes that some nice jolly person like Maxine Reese were doing all the announcing of Jimmy's virtues. Jimmy Carter may be eminently trustworthy, by comparison (at least by comparison?) with other political figures of modern times. He does seem to genuinely think he is trustworthy. But you would like to hear Maxine rather than Jimmy saying it. If she said it, we could assess him on the merits. But—and here lies one of the problems the smarter journalists have to face—Jimmy Carter, as chief spokesman for his campaign, as the man who carries the banner, has assigned himself also the role of chief announcer of his own trustworthiness. Now trustworthiness is right at the head of the Boy Scout catalogue of virtues ("a Scout is trustworthy, loyal, helpful, friendly, courteous, kind . . ."). Trustworthiness is also the kind of virtue most adults inculcate in their children, if indeed they teach virtue at all—while they, of course, write a fat bill of special rights, reserve a wide area of arbitrary interpretation, for themselves.

Anyhow, Jimmy Carter's proclamation of his own trustworthiness, like his insistence on his own Best-ness (well, why not the — the Best?) comes hard upon the ears, tuned to flim-flam, of most journalists—and most of the rest of us. Good grief! Is this guy trumpeting his own moral

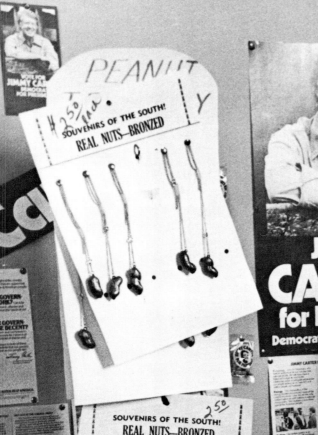

excellence? This is something even a mother would find a bit much. As Jimmy's own mother Lillian is supposed to have said to him once, when he was yet again proclaiming his never-greater love of his wife Rosalynn, his born-again Christianness, and his unwillingness to tell a lie: Jimmy, there are some things you don't have to go around saying.

Yet Jimmy Carter is aware that the virtue of trustworthiness is hardly to be taken for granted in a politician today—with the spectacle of Watergate so warm in our memory. One does get the impression sometimes that Jimmy is, or wished he were, saying these things about someone else—about God, maybe? But he says that he is good—and it seems he is getting away with it. After all, some people reason: Is there anyone as well qualified as Jimmy to know exactly what he is like? That is, apart from Rosalynn, who has been playing the role of precursor—with the greatest possible grace and conviction. And of course, people make allowances. There is the ragged old saying, "He who tooteth not his own horn, the same shall not be tooted." When people come to hear a politician, they expect some self-advertisement.

Still and all, it is a relief to hear other voices speaking up for him now. It was nice to see and hear old Mo Udall, after all that had gone on, say, "He beat us fair and square . . . This is a good man, Jimmy Carter, and he will make a

strong President, and I am behind him." The advent of Walter Mondale may help. Mondale seems to be a true if sudden convert to Jimmy Carter. (And among the chosen few, well, isn't Fritz Mondale precisely the fellow easiest to regard as the best of all—not just as a candidate but as a man?) Anyway, Grits' own Fritz does take some of the messianic burden off Wee Jimmy's shoulders. "Jimmy Carter is very bright," says Mondale. "He has done a lot of work, and I like the way he attacks problems. Most politicians, I regret to say, begin with polls and then back into a solution after they've analyzed what may be popular . . . In our discussions we talked about problems first on their own merit . . . One thing that appeals to Democrats—he's shown a lot of courage on civil rights. Here's a man who looks honest, looks decent, looks like he can manage, looks like he's not full of himself and looks like he's free. He doesn't have any entangling interests that control him . . .

"Carter is still not well known. While the polls indicate that he has very strong appeal in a general sense, I think there is also a softness there that has to be dealt with, and I think he understands. I think that is partly the skepticism of our age. They test all of us. They expect we are all liars and cheaters or abductors, and it takes a while for a new public personality coming out of a unique environment to sell himself . . ."

Of course Jimmy's own tone is an asset to him. This lull of low-key Jimmy talk becomes a problem for the Jimmy critics. It does not stir public anger. The man speaks softly—at times still almost in a kind of a mumble. Jimmy is not shouting his virtues, only quietly talking about them. Others might, in other voices, rouse public hostility, but from this man you do not actually expect great things—only confident and competent performance. I was a competent Governor, the soft voice seems to be saying; I will be a competent President. The tone itself does not convey any more than that. It is impossible to see him as extravagant. He doesn't even seem to be abnormally ambitious. The mind which moves the voice may envision a historic presidential performance that will be vastly more than competent. But to the people he is not making wild claims.

This soft voice brings us back to South Georgia. In the past its heat fired the demagogues—and those poor whites, desperate for any kind of hope, who listened to the demagogues. But that heat, working in quiet Plains on a mind of Jimmy Carter's caliber, has had a tempering effect. Oh, you do feel that the fire within will be ready next time Jimmy needs it. But anyone can hear his prevailing tone of calm reasonableness, can see that the dominant disposition is a willingness for long thoughtful conversation out of which useful reflection may come at any turn. Jimmy Carter not only is not a demagogue; he is the opposite of a demagogue. He is a lifelong gentleman, in many ways a shy man, distrustful of arrogant emotion—in himself or anyone else. His friend John Pope has said that Jimmy has always been "able to do with words what somebody else might try to do with their fists." He seems not to be vindictive. Not for him the Kennedy motto: "Don't get mad, get even." He sees it as a "temptation to judge other people without charity," and the judge within comes down hard on him whenever he is inclined to thoughts in that direction. His religious nature does not allow him to nurse his wrath to keep it warm. This

lack of rancor in him is one of the reasons he has become reconciler of Robert Strauss's reconciliation-minded Democratic party.

But can we really trust Jimmy Carter? Isn't Jimmy Carter dishonest? Well, there's his book WHY NOT THE BEST?—it's honest in more ways than one. It's a fair presentation of the man—who can show profound human understanding, who can quote Dylan Thomas appropriately, yet who is also capable of wince-making lapses in literary taste (in a Fourth of July speech) in comparing on an equal basis the pop historian Will Durant with Arnold Toynbee, the author of A STUDY OF HISTORY. In the book there are all kinds of styles, as there are all kinds of moods in a human being. There is some pretty fine narrative, and some weaker narrative. The book is not superficial, but some passages are filled with the clumsy jargon of one or another science. There are passages of inspired reflection. There is good and bad speechifying, plodding and vigorous writing, there are awkard and fine turns of phrase. The tone is sad as well as optimistic—although in it lamentation becomes hope.

But the thing is this: the whole strange medley was actually writ by hand—by Jimmy's hand—in hotel rooms, on airplanes, in odd moments at his desk and on his own typewriter at home. There is no ghost writer here, no shadow even of a good editor's pencil; and this makes it an authentic communication of the man himself. It is a splendid source to keep turning to, for anyone who wants to find out what Jimmy Carter is like. You find him talking vividly about disagreements with his wife. He also talks about the unimportance to Plains of his return home after the Navy years, about his loading hundred-pound bags of fertilizer onto farmers' trucks. On page after page you find evidence of an innocence in Jimmy Carter—and this despite all of his considerable experience. Jimmy is, in the book, as honest as Job.

Where then do we get all this stuff about his dishonesty? Well, probably all the calculated cosmetic effort—which Jimmy appears to take with the same strange childlike innocent acceptance as he does so much else in life—contributes to this. And he asks for criticism, begs for it. Because he will say he is honest and that he won't lie—never. But he will—when he feels he has to—avoid, deviate, duck, dodge, escape, slip or twist away. He's an old shifty hips, Jimmy is, and if he's got a mine field to run through—well, Jimmy may be innocent, but he's no fool.

All right, let's try again. Jimmy Carter is certainly not honest if measured against a kind of mathematical model or angelic mode of honesty. No human being is as honest as all that. We all have to be very shrewd and swift at times—in a sinful world. Not only is Jimmy no exception to this, but he has far more tightrope walking to do than almost any of us. The words put into the mouth of Sir Thomas More, the great Roman Catholic jurist, explain it all well enough: "God made the angels to show him splendor—as he made the animals for their innocence and plants for their simplicity. But Man he made to serve him wittily, in the tangle of his mind . . . Our natural business lies in escaping."

Mirrors? Well, move the mirrors slightly, and you see that Jimmy's wily cunning combines with a natural and Baptist reticence. He is both willing to admit to his religious faith, and reluctant to talk about it. For Baptists, as Miz

Lillian says, "It's a matter between you and God." Yet this motivation is at the bottom of everything. "The most important thing in my life is Jesus Christ"—that's the key to Jimmy Carter! To the whole question of just how really sincere he is! But you are not going to get him to make a spectacle of himself by discussing the content of that Jesus-relationship. If you understand, fine. If you don't, well, he is willing to say what he thinks the Bible teaches about the oughts and shouldn't oughts of life. But his own inner life is essentially a private affair. He really has to be somewhat opaque in this very personal area. How to get at the heart of that question of honesty? No way, not a-tall. You have to take him on faith. On faith? Yep. This Jimmy Carter is the limit. Nobody like our Jimmy, before or since.

Sometimes you wish he would not even talk about his honesty. By his deft use of language, his subtlety, he sometimes comes out sounding dishonest precisely because—unlike the other politicians—his mind is always functioning. But in the end you have to agree that he is right in stressing this quality, even in the face of the lumpen literal-minded intellectual proletariat of our era. Just compare him to those other politicians. For instance, a year or two from now, let's see what has happened to Jimmy's campaign promises—the projects he talked about in his convention acceptance speech. If you don't like those promises, probably best to vote against him. Because when he says about tax reform, "It's gonna happen: you can depend on it," you'd better believe you can depend on it. And so on with all those projects like zero-base budgeting and welfare reform and government reorganization which are main-line projects with Jimmy. Consider this: THE ATLANTA CONSTITUTION is published in the city which of all cities knows Jimmy most intimately. Most of the real Carter critics live in and around Atlanta. Now the editors of that newspaper, who in 1970 favored Carl Sanders and opposed Jimmy for Governor, in March 1976 printed the following statement: "The main thing perhaps to be said about James Earl Carter's public record in Georgia . . . is simply that his record can be examined in detail and it bears scrutiny. He was an honest, competent, innovative chief executive of a large state and he filled those responsibilities with distinction."

So Jimmy Carter's basic honesty, his basic willingness to face what he is and to tell you what he is and also keep you up to date, seem extraordinary in any comparison to normal politicians. And the book! Any self-respecting ghost writer would have glossed over maybe half of what Jimmy brings forward. Even when he produces something in his own favor, Jimmy usually manages to keep his weakness or insufficiency or ordinariness sharply in perspective. And if the ordinariness is matched in fact with a brilliance of mind (manifested especially in judgment and decision), it is all there, and the reader is not being gulled, as with the fictions contrived by an Eisenhower's various ghosts.

Now, one has to admit that it would be difficult to construct a better background for Jimmy Carter's purposes than the barefoot-boy-to-governor, the outhouse-to-White House scenario that Jimmy's working with. Yet his background is his in fact. All right, much of it suggests, at first, decency to the point of dullness, a boring kind of small-town American ethical correctness. At first. Yet a reader trying hard to be objective about it nevertheless has to conclude that the goodness and decency isn't boring at all, in the end—not in Jimmy's case. Because it is precisely this plain living and high thinking, according to conventional ethical standards, that is now making Jimmy a wonder for the revelation of the nation, and a stumbling block for the consternation of Republicans. All the plain values that those decent Republicans, the small-town middle American folk, are supposed to stand for, Jimmy does in fact stand for, and in spades and royal flushes—this man who is also the candidate of the black mothers of America.

Moreover, this blameless and exemplary life did not bore Jimmy. The standards and principles he stuck by were, to him, the vein and mother lode of a life richly lived and constantly discovered—over against the drift in American values. And even now this life rises and builds toward a breathtakingly promising future. Anyway, there are going to be useful lessons here not only for understanding Jimmy but for the guidance of all the rest of us. You can depend on it.

Strange! That on the campaign trail with Jimmy, journalists talk about subjects like traditional religion and religious faith, and moral values and the spiritual condition of the country, and ask weird unanswerable questions about whether Jimmy in his heart of hearts is a hypocrite, or just a politician of higher quality than others, or whether he is some kind of Christian saint-in-the-making. (Well, he sure isn't there yet, and he'd be the first to tell you that, and his mother Lillian Carter a close second.)

Who is he? Well, try to work through some of the paradoxes of this Jimmy life. He is perhaps the most complex man to involve himself in presidential politics in our lifetime, and maybe the least complicated. He is the most conventional candidate in memory, with the most unconventional candidacy. He seems possessed both of vaulting ambition and complete religious detachment. He is a man of dramatic initiatives, yet of an almost aggressive passivity (a double whammy right there). He is a whole-souled pragmatist, with what seems to be a palpable vision of American greatness. He is a man with a mysterious inaccessible inner life in which, it is claimed, Jesus Christ is alive and in control; yet he is a cold-eyed, systematic, relentlessly sane technician of progress.

Jimmy Carter is an honest-to-God social liberal who is an authentic fiscal conservative; a man of deep commitment who, when asked in New Hampshire whether he was a leftist or a rightist or a moderate, could say: I don't have to declare myself, so I won't. He is a gracious victor who is a driving taskmaster. He is stubborn yet soft, bossman yet servant, a total participant who is a coolly objective observer. He is completely out in the open, and more and more so all the time—yet sly and wily as the serpent. And once again, there is that innocence and that experience— the crafty, calculating pro politician who is as impressionable and gee-whiz as a seven year old boy.

He's not easy to figure out, this Jimmy Carter. He wants to win, he has a will to win, but he seems to lack the will to power. He's competitive. But he thinks of victory as an achievement to be won by sweet reason, hard work, civil discourse, and a firm belief that love (in the Southern sense of concern, compassion, affection) is the answer to problems among human beings. He doesn't for a moment want to be a loser. But winning isn't everything for Jimmy. He describes believably how he could pull himself together even after ruinous defeat. But "you show me a good loser," he says, "and I will show you—a loser."

Now most people are losers. In the presidential election, all the Democrats defeated by Jimmy Carter, and all the Republicans about to be driven into exile by Jimmy Carter, and all their armies of retainers and henchmen and hangers-on, their spear-carriers and pillow-carriers, are rendered by Jimmy Carter—losers. And most of them don't like it, not a-tall. So they yell. And they holler. And they complain about him. Anybody who has come up so fast, they say, come on so strong—however quiet and civil he may appear—has got to have something wrong with him. If they do not watch him and complain about him, what will he do in the night? Once he is elected? Power!

Well, a visitor to the Carter homeland, who meets Jimmy and the family, who listens both to Jimmy and to what the homefolk have to say about him, does not perceive him as mad for power, or a pursuer of power for its own sake. There is every possibility Jimmy Carter is not a power-pursuer at all. He wants to be President, because he thinks the presidency is an office he can honorably fill. Does that sound too smooth? Well, that—or so it seems to the observer—is the sum total of what Jimmy Carter is up to. If concern and compassion are so to be orchestrated that they be translated into simple justice, then—in Jimmy Carter's view—there is no better conductor of the orchestra than Jimmy. But the grasping for power as such—in the sense familiar from the experience of Lyndon Johnson's manipulation of the levers of power and his "yore President" Godfatherism ("Son, they're all my helicopters"), or Richard Nixon's vindictive use of power (breaking and entering; the enemies list) seem entirely alien to the motives that operate in Jimmy Carter.

In fact, part of what makes Jimmy hard to understand is his constantly falling back from partisanship. Yes, he is sometimes temperamental. And he is devious, crafty, adept, opportunistic, calculating, competitive and determined—and a very tough in-fighter. But he is not a hater. He is in fact, in some degree honest and truthful and open and candid and concerned and compassionate, as well as competent and efficient. More than that, where he is deficient in the nobler qualities, he sees the weakness in himself and constantly tries to adjust and improve his performance. He does not want to create ill will. He wants to avoid violent emotion. He is a trying-hard Christian. It's a "high and perfect standard" that the Bible offers, he says. Difficult for him to live up to, as for any man.

It seems, then, that if Jimmy is in appearance sometimes a phony, he is probably a phony phony. It is possible that he is not only real, but a lot realer than most of us suspect. One problem, if it can be called a problem, is that Jimmy is not only going to be the President, but he is going to carry his main brain trust on his own shoulders. We're not used to this. History, especially recent history, has not prepared us. It is as though some hillbilly (a seed peanut breeder?), with no help at all from Harvard or Yale, had set himself up as adviser to the President. The added peculiarity is that he also is setting himself up as President: He wants—and he may be able—to be not only his own Henry Kissinger, but his own man.

Okay. Let's get it all out on the table. In Jimmy Carter as President the taxpayer is getting—what? We're going to lay out two hundred great big ones a year for salary. Then there are the allowances, plus retirement, plus benefits, plus tens of millions of dollars in aides, extras, helicopters and Air Force One. So! What use is Jimmy Carter to us?

Well, he's a laborer. He's an administrator. He's a businessman. He's a long-range government planner. He's a nuclear engineer. He's an election expert. He's a social thinker and critic. He's an inventor: a structural and social inventor capable of creating surprises. (This presidency could be interesting to watch.) He brings to his work the inventor's and engineer's and scientist's and reforming critic's dissatisfaction with the status quo. And he's an exceptionally able financial manager. He could without doubt make a very good living managing assets. He is also a concerned and compassionate human being, and very anxious to translate concern and compassion into public policy. He is a man of religious and moral principle who admits he falls short of what he ought to be. Yet he is and will be a moral leader. He is a student, and an omnivorous reader— one of the most educable men ever to approach the White House. He is also a politician—perhaps the most brilliant of our era, yet one who has mistakes enough of his own to learn from.

All this expertise of Jimmy's has presidential implications. For example, he is very much concerned with targeting. "As a planner and a businessman and chief executive," he says, "I know from experience that uncertainty is also a devastating affliction in private life and government." He recalls the biblical saying: "If the trumpet give an uncertain sound, who shall prepare himself to the battle?" He knows the importance of purpose in society.

As a nuclear engineer, with advanced courses in nuclear physics, and as a former atomic submarine officer, he knows and has personal access to more information about nuclear weaponry than any other politician. He can think and talk vividly about the hideous destructive potential of the arsenal. "When we talk about forty megaton capability for our submarines or eight hundred megatons for our bomber fleet . . . in human terms this is an unbelievable amount of death." He knows, at first hand, what a nuclear strike would mean to submarine crewmen carrying out the orders . . .

Jimmy Carter has what amounts almost to a devotion to unremitting toil and labor. He loves hard work, and the accomplishment that often follows. He has always felt, says his wife Rosalynn, that "no matter what you started to do, you did the best job you could do. He tried to instill it in our children, and I think he succeeded."

And they are persistent, these Carter people. Jimmy's Uncle Alton says: "I'll tell you what the reputation of the Carters is. Every one of them—every one of them's been known of—has been hard-headed as the devil. They're not switch and switchabout. They're not here today and gone tomorrow. That's the kind of folk the Carters are. Every Carter I've ever known was like that. That's the whole truth."

He has labored very hard all his life, this fellow Jimmy Carter, and—whatever else can be said about him—it is certain that he won't be found spending his presidency on ski slopes or golf courses. And Rosalynn Carter! She is not simply his wife. She is a heavily and deeply involved co-laborer. Henry V's words could be hers, with her rare warm reflectiveness, set in soft steel.

> Let me speak proudly: tell the constable
> We are but warriors for the working-day;
> Our gayness and our gilt are all besmirch'd
> With rainy marching in the painful field . . .

There is, perhaps as never before, a sense of an earned presidency—and a hard-earned first ladyship as well.

What about Jimmy Carter's religion? Jimmy's not a religious fanatic, any more than he's a demagogue. Nor does he come on as some kind of messiah or savior. Jimmy's never been an object of veneration, in Atlanta or Plains or anywhere else, and does not seem interested at all in worshipful crowd reaction. In fact he still blushes with embarrassment when black evangelical congregations respond warmly to him. He seems pleased enough with what success he's earned, and is delighted with the overcoming of the more gross prejudices against him. But, he's not especially demonstrative about even this—just goes on to the next thing. And his Sunday school teaching focuses, quietly and with considerable sophistication, not on Jimmy himself, but on the biblical text he's dealing with.

What kind of religious man is he? His mother says, "Jimmy's a hard down Baptist Christian. Sensible. And deep." He talks about religious living in terms of search and struggle. Jimmy Carter is a believer. He goes to church on Sunday, but religious faith is not the same as church on Sunday. Faith is something else—a leap into darkness. Faith—real faith—involves an effort to get in touch with, and to live life in terms of, a mysterious Presence in the universe, greater than ourselves. This effort, in Jimmy's case, brings with it a rigorous and profound self-criticism. It can also bring to bear a sense of the majesty of the Other, and of the human other, that can provide strong sustenance to the life of compassion, the life of commitment, in ways that are strange to most human beings.

> Suffer us not to mock ourselves with falsehood
> Teach us to care and not to care
> Teach us to sit still
> Even among these rocks,
> Our peace in His will
> And even among these rocks . . .
> Suffer me not to be separated
>
> And let my cry come unto Thee . . .

Jimmy Carter believes in social reform, along lines set out in careful long-range plans. He's not an issues man. He's a targets and projects man. Action, not explanation, is what mainly interests him. "Our nation now," he says, "has no understandable national purpose, no clearly defined goals, and no organizational mechanism to develop or achieve such purposes or goals . . . What is our national policy for the production, acquisition, distribution, or consumption of energy in times of shortage or doubtful supply? There is no policy! What are our long-range goals in health care, transportation, land use, economic development, waste disposal, or housing? There are no goals! . . .

"A government that is honest and competent, with clear purpose and strong leadership, can work with the American people to meet the challenges of the present and the future."

It is political rhetoric, but the critique seems fair, and the tone appropriate. There have been political critiques before, and the critic, once in office, has for one reason or another not been able to do much about them. Jimmy is an optimist, a positive thinker, a problem solver. American optimism has been wrong before, positive thinking has gone haywire for us before; problems have often yielded before to cures far worse then the disease.

There are limits, in the circumstances, on what Jimmy Carter can do, but not a lot of limits; in the circumstances, actually, immense national and global and human possibilities. The compassion and concern are very important here. They serve as values against which what the builder builds will be measured in the long run of history.

There are also great presidencies which Jimmy Carter will eventually be measured against. George Washington, with Alexander Hamilton's help, made the presidency of the United States a strong but not an imperial office. Thomas Jefferson demonstrated brilliant party leadership in working effectively with Congress. Andrew Jackson made the office responsive to the will of the people as well as to his own. Abraham Lincoln, moving with matchless confidence and intelligence and imagination, made the presidency an instrument of power in crisis. Theodore Roosevelt used it as a "bully pulpit" to carry issues to the people and gain support for humanly significant projects. Woodrow Wilson solidified presidential power as the prime mover of legislative action. Franklin D. Roosevelt used his presidency to lead the country from ruin to prosperity, and exercised unexampled international influence. John Kennedy brought a broad public sense of identification with the presidency. With Lyndon Johnson it became in instrument of unprecedented social change. There were, however, deficiencies in all these presidencies; and American history yields many more weak presidents than strong ones.

What makes a great presidency? The strong presidents have or develop a vision of the office. They must either respond strongly to crisis (as did Lincoln and FDR) or act decisively for change that is in the public interest (as did Theodore Roosevelt). They cannot make major mistakes (as did Lyndon Johnson and Richard Nixon). In the presidency, a strong national image counts for something (Washington); adept party and congressional leadership counts (Jefferson); a strong sense of purpose counts (Andrew Jackson); intelligence counts (Wilson); compassion counts (Lincoln). Practicality is important, as are maturity and flexibility of response. Commitment, hard work, and vision are of the essence.

What can we expect from the Jimmy years? Jimmy Carter has said that he is as interested as anyone in seeing what kind of president he'll be.

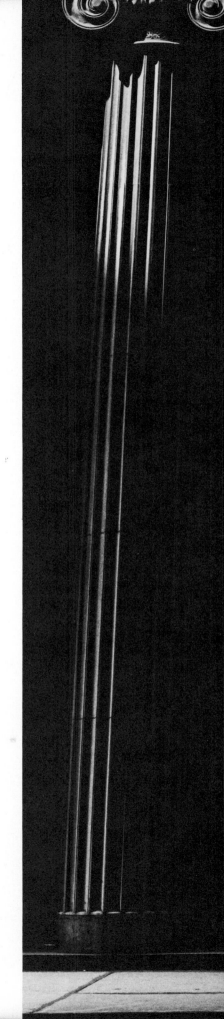